FRAYLE
Skin & Sorrow

ALR033

Published by

Aqualamb

FRAYLE:
Gwyn Strang
Sean Bilovecky
Jason Knotek
Jon Vinson

CREDITS:
All songs written by Frayle except "Brights Eyes" written by Frayle and King Midnight.

Recorded, mixed and mastered at the Doom Tower.

Frayle plays Orange Amps

Cover Photo: Frayle
Photos: Jeremy Saffer
Live Photos: Lena Knotek
All other Photos: Frayle
Book Design & Illustrations: Aqualamb and Frayle
with layout & illustration assistance from Gregory Tolstikov

We would like to thank:
Jeannette Strang, John Strang, Karen Strang, Uriel, Remiel, Luna, Nina Bilovecky, Virginia Bilovecky, Marsha Craft, Ryan Bilovecky, Mike Callahan, Désirée Hanssen, Johnathan Swafford, Eric Palmerlee, Nathan Offerdahl, John Neely, John O Kay, Tyler Hodges, Carl Schultz, Ella Stormark, Mona Miluski, Aaron Gray, Jason Knotek, Barrett Close, Lena Knotek, JoAnne Ginley, McKayla Ginley, Ryan Ginley, Katherine, Emma, Briar, Earthquaker Devices, various plants, and everyone who has supported us on this journey.

First Printing: Edition of 500
ISBN: 979-8-9857365-4-0

frayleband.com
aqualamb.org

CONTENTS

FRAYLE – SKIN & SORROW

Treacle and Revenge	25
Bright Eyes	39
Skin & Sorrow	55
Ipecac	67
Stars	77
Roses	87
Sacrifant	105
All The Things I Was	119
Song For The Dead	131
Perfect Wound	145

The music for Frayle – *Skin & Sorrow*
can be downloaded
via the link below:

http://aqualamb.org/033

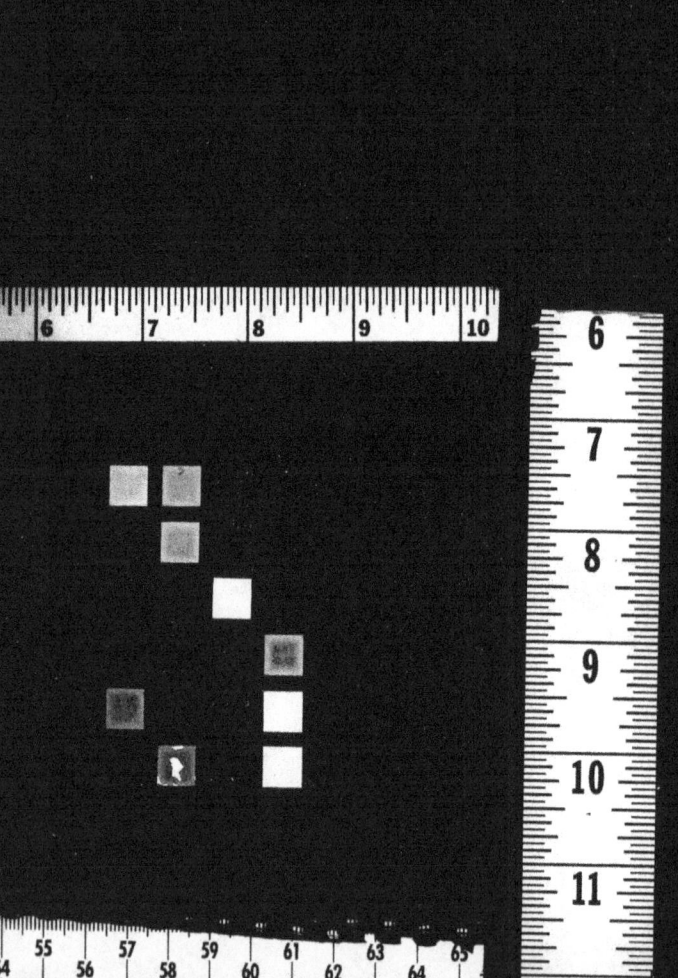

THE
National Garment Cutter

BOOK OF DIAGRAMS.

STRANG & BILOVECKY AND CO.

PROPRIETORS.

666 WEST LAKE STREET,

CLEVELAND, OHIO

AGENTS WANTED

FRAYLE
Skin & Sorrow

SKIN & SORROW

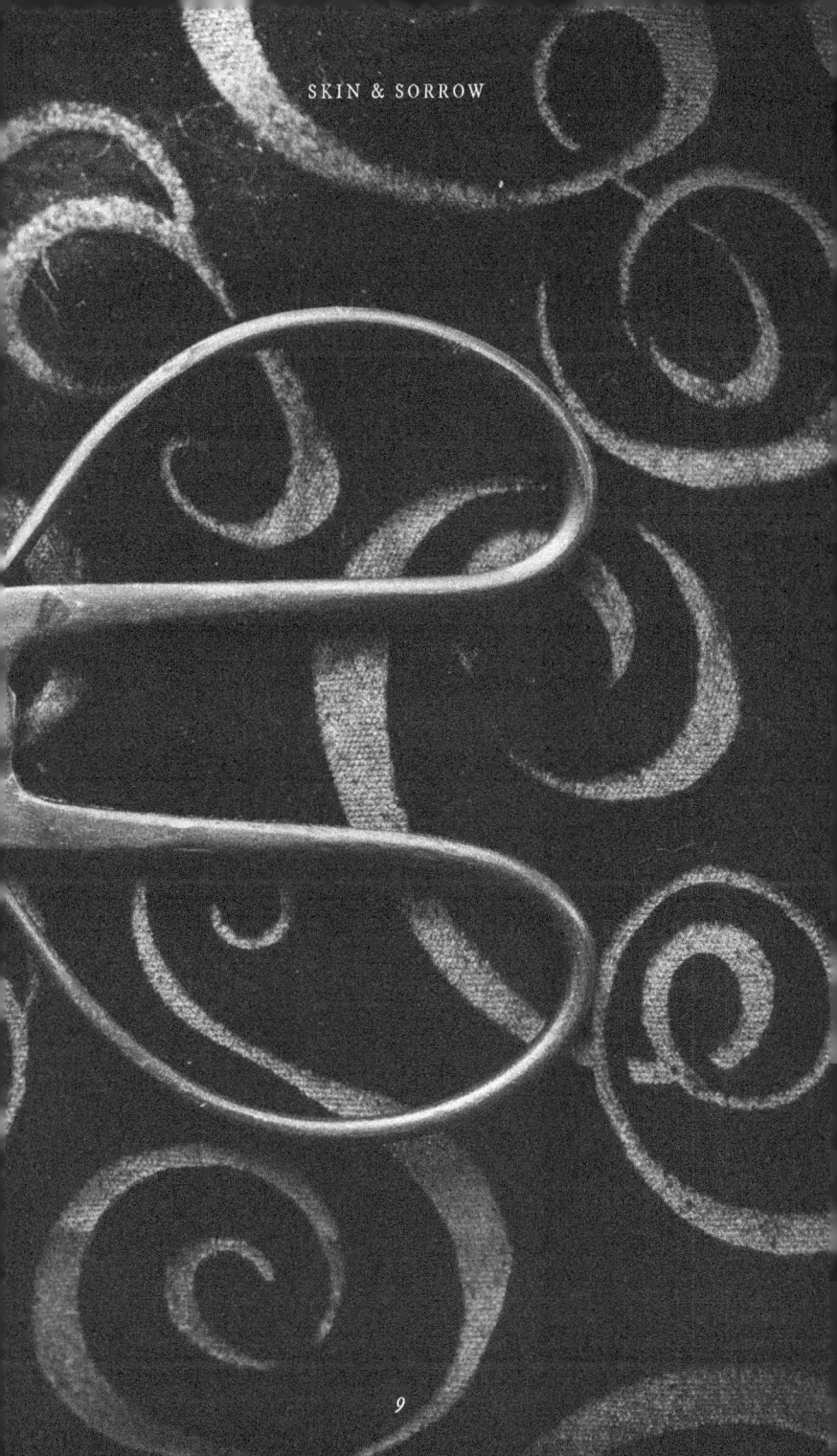

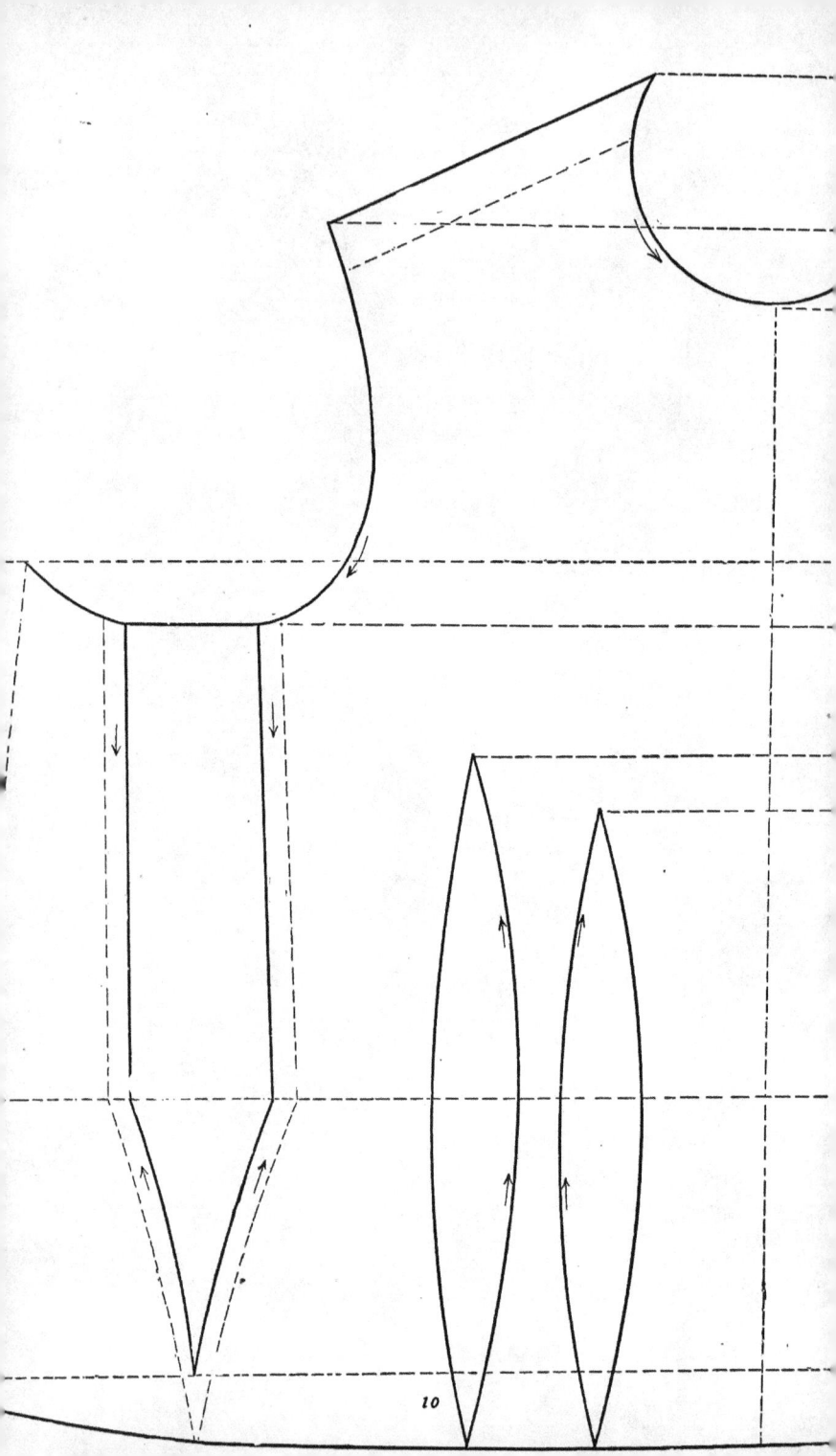

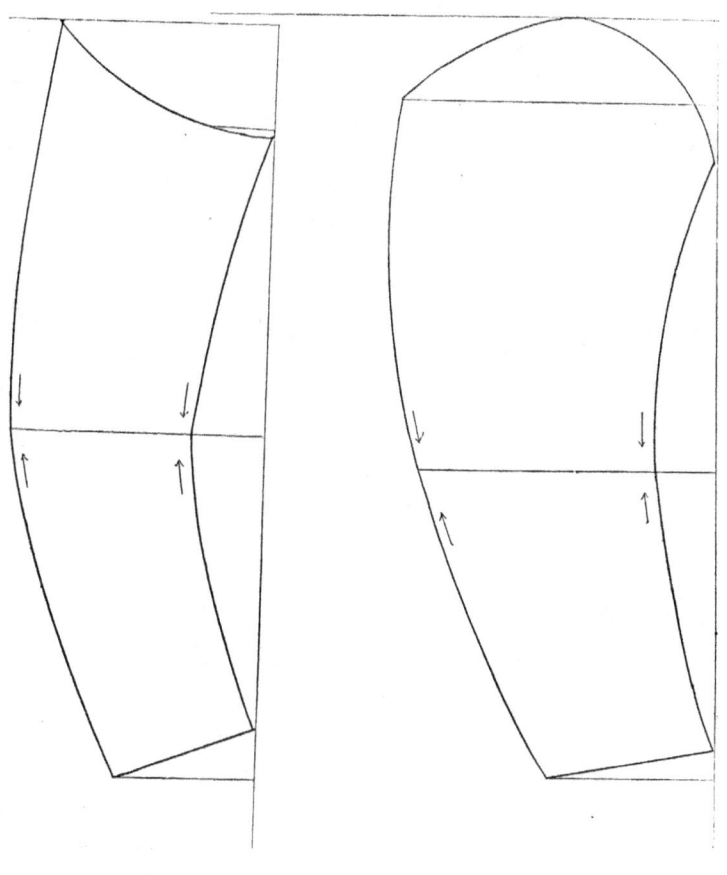

SKIN & SORROW

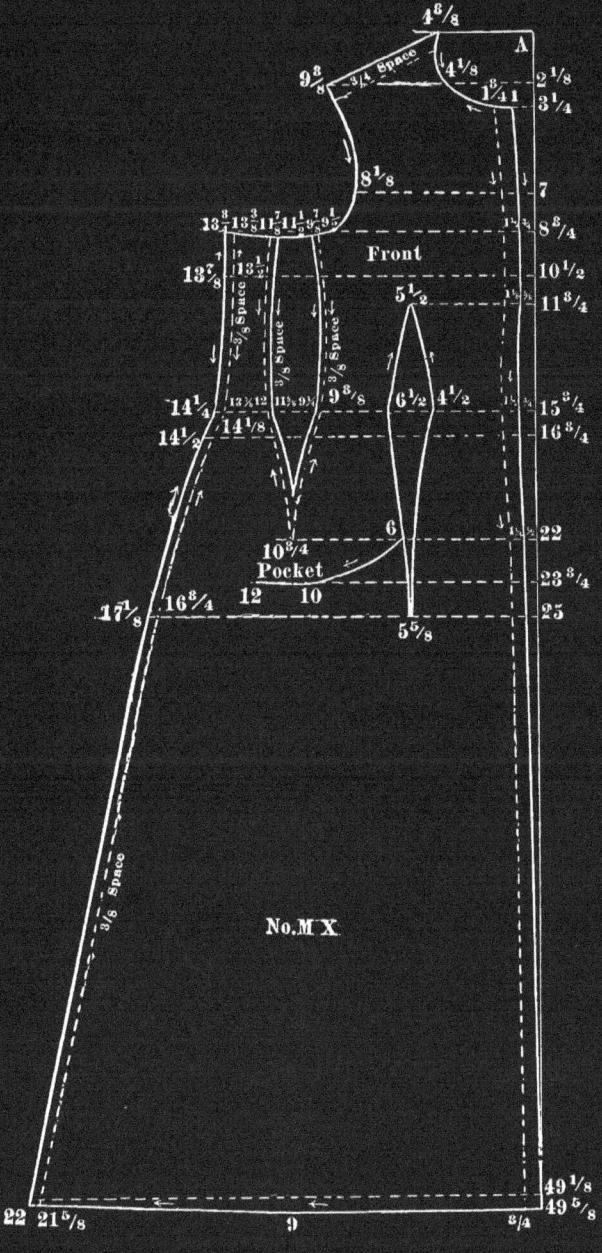

SKIN & SORROW

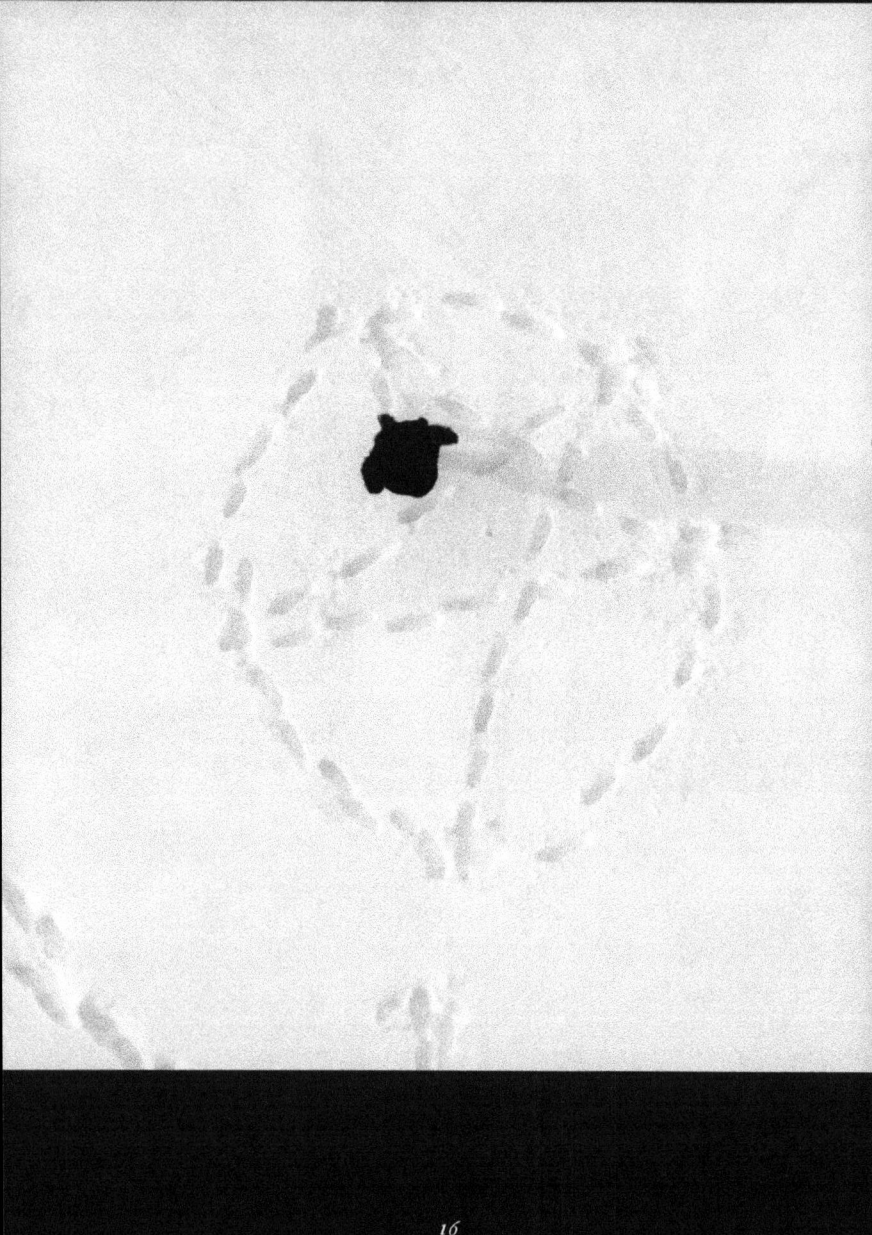

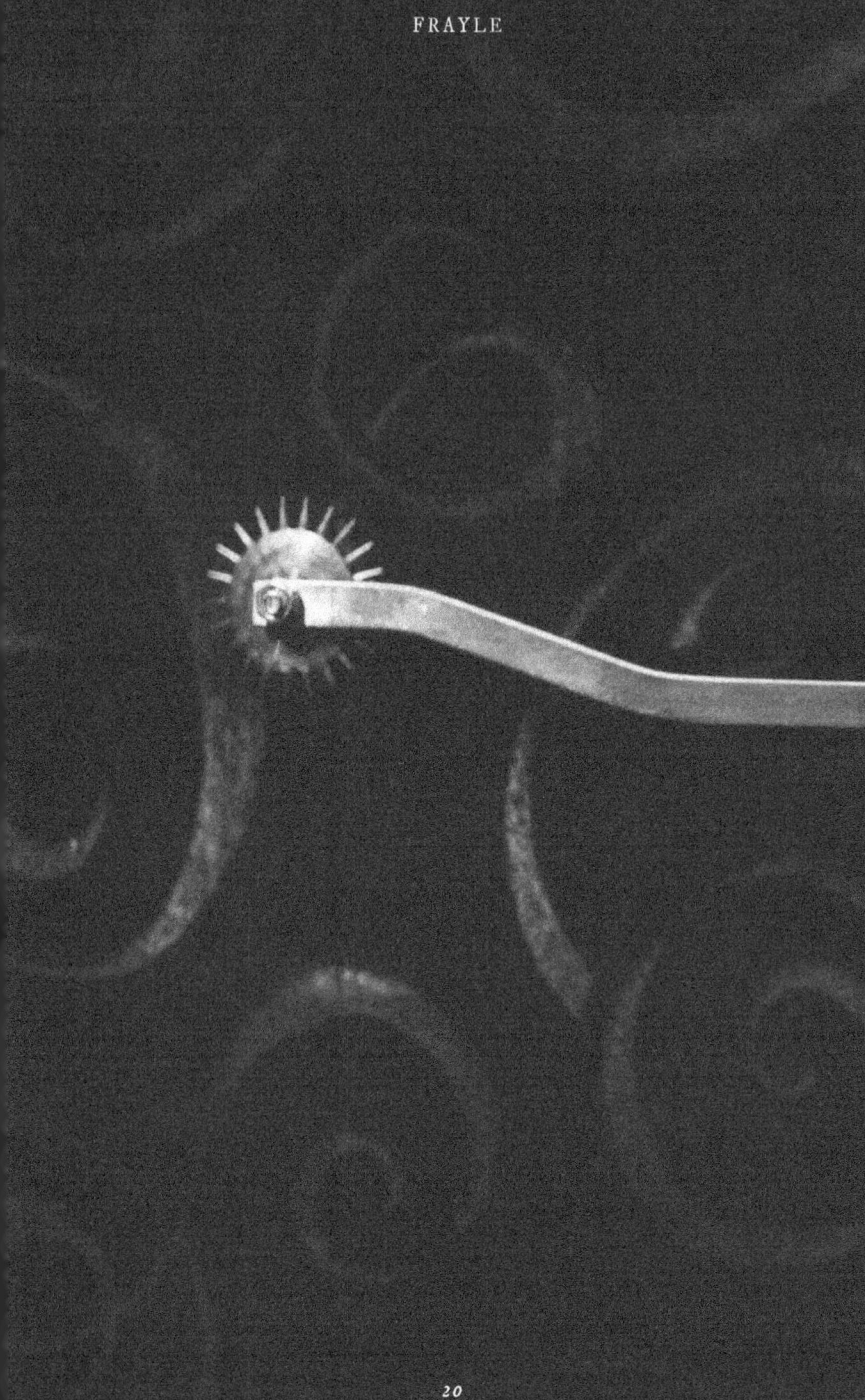

SKIN & SORROW

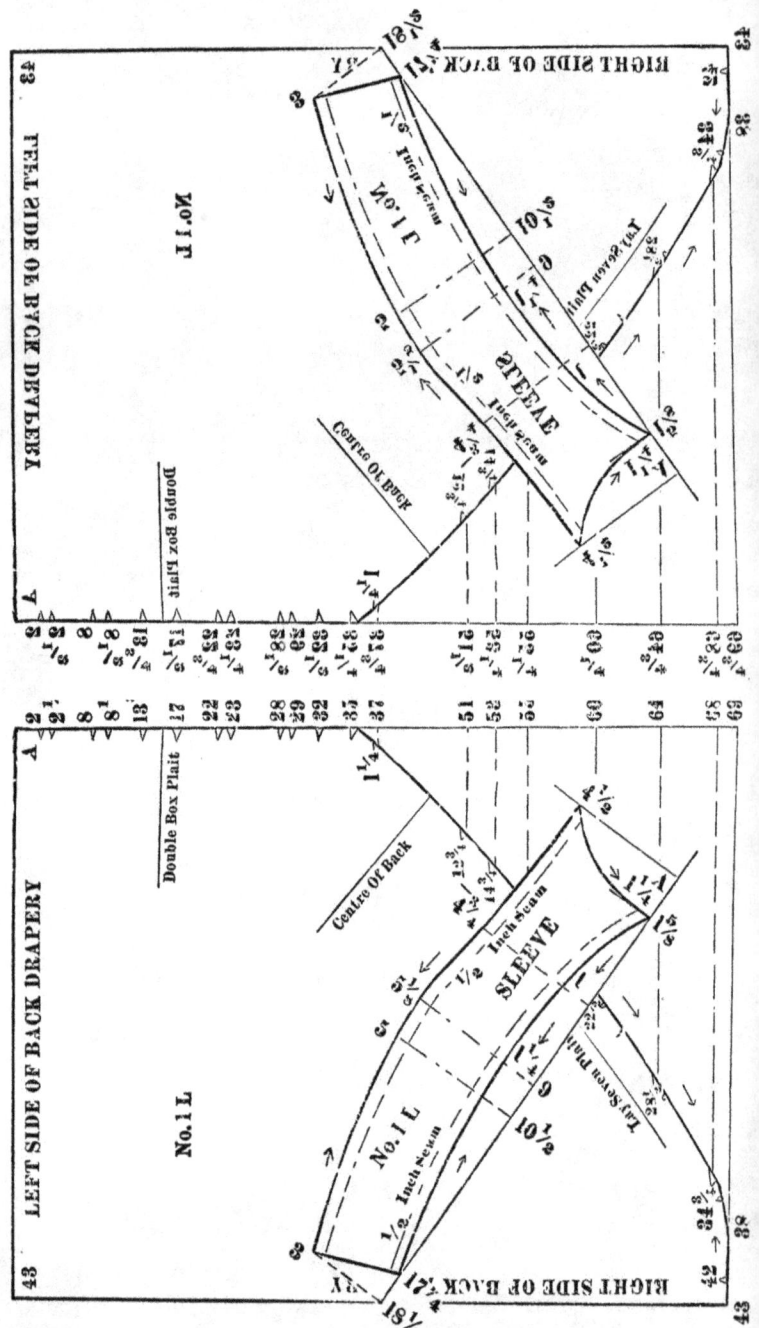

SKIN & SORROW

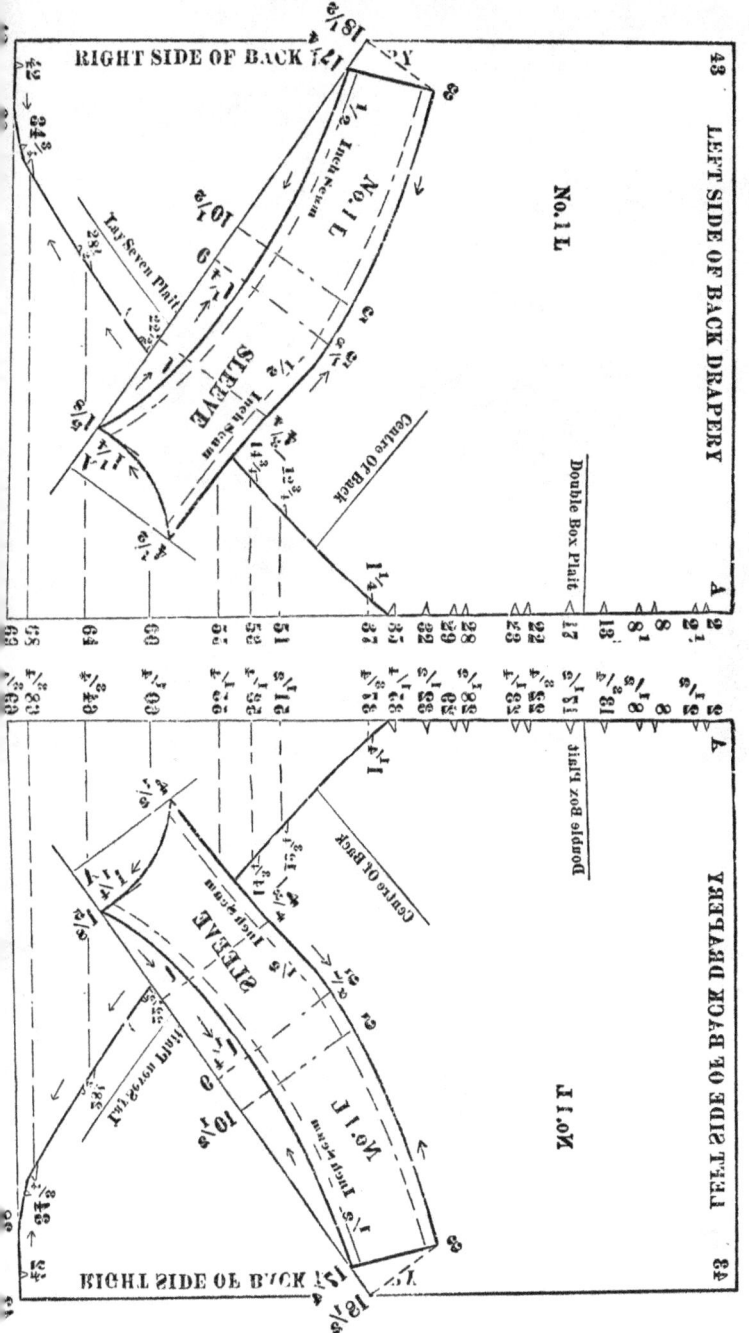

FRAYLE

Treacle & Revenge

Would you die for me like you promised?
Such sweetness.

So tired of this treacle. Hold you to your truth.
So bored of empty words.
I will have Revenge!

You promised to love me forever.
Whatever.

So tired of this treacle. Hold you to your truth.
So bored with empty words.
I will have Revenge!

Now I'm the tragedy that I tried to avoid.
Your words, your lies, such pretty noise.
The things you say, they bring such callous joy
Rip through my heart & left to fill the void.

Pretty lies told. Why should I believe?
Pretty lies told. Why should I believe?

Now I'm the tragedy that I tried to avoid.
Your words, your lies, such pretty noise.
The things you say, they bring such callous joy
Rip through my heart & left to fill a void.

FRAYLE

SKIN & SORROW

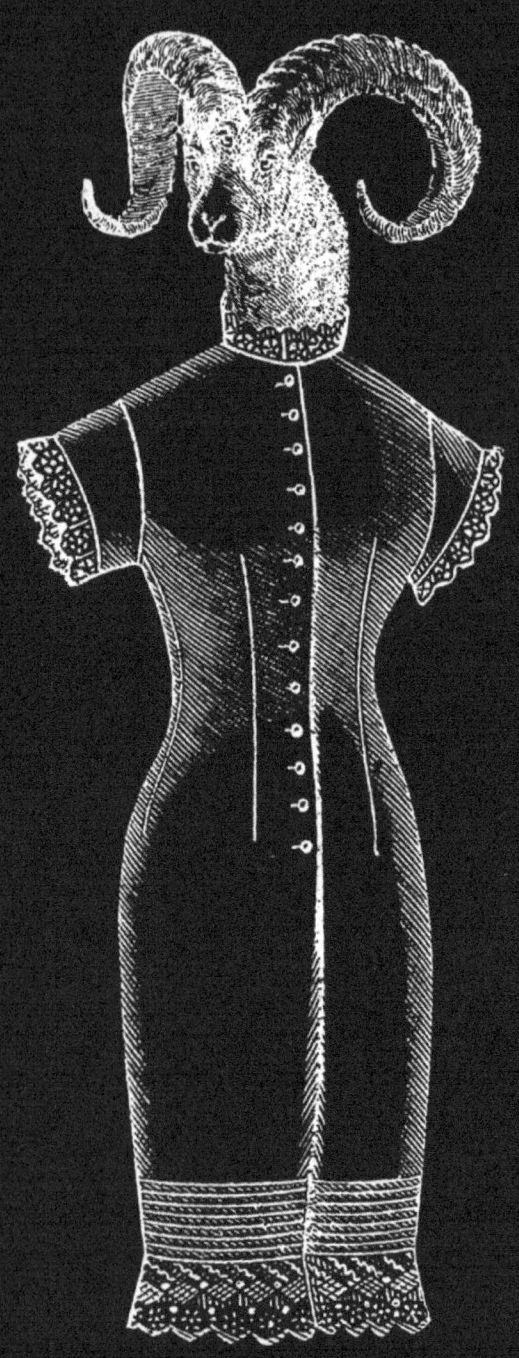

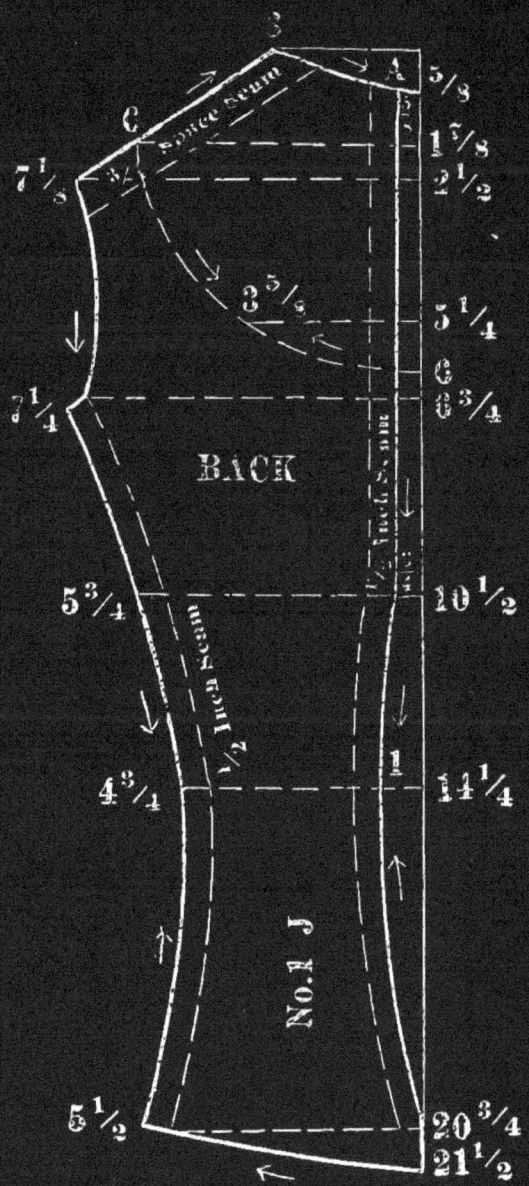

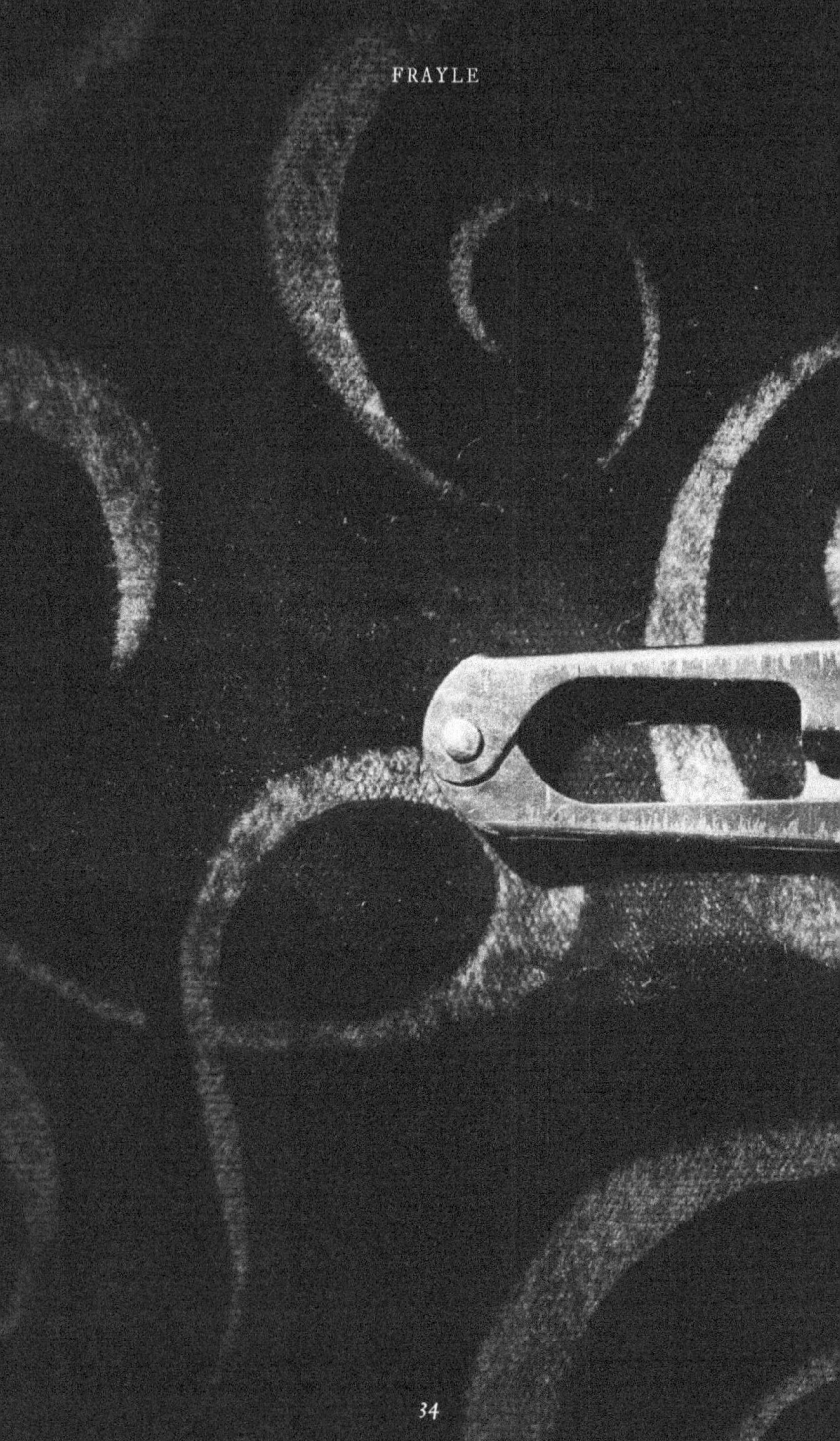

SKIN & SORROW

FRAYLE

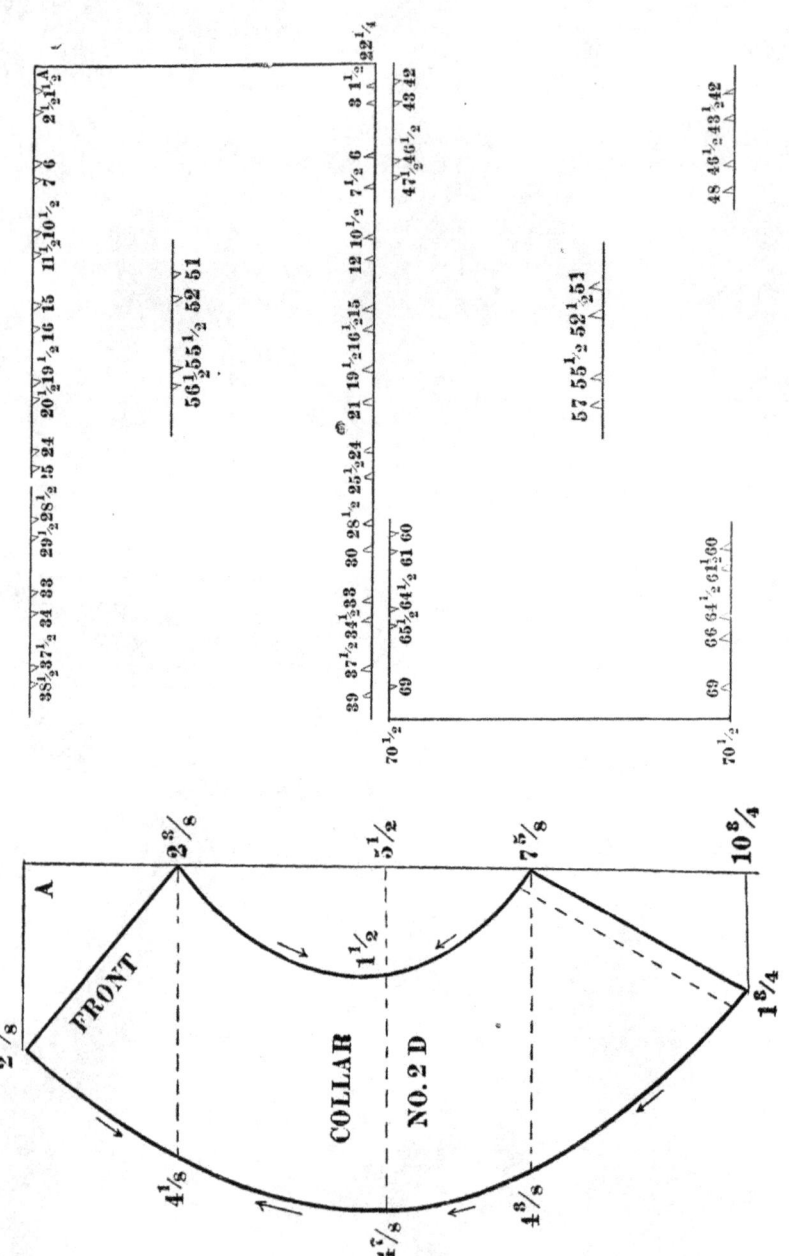

SKIN & SORROW

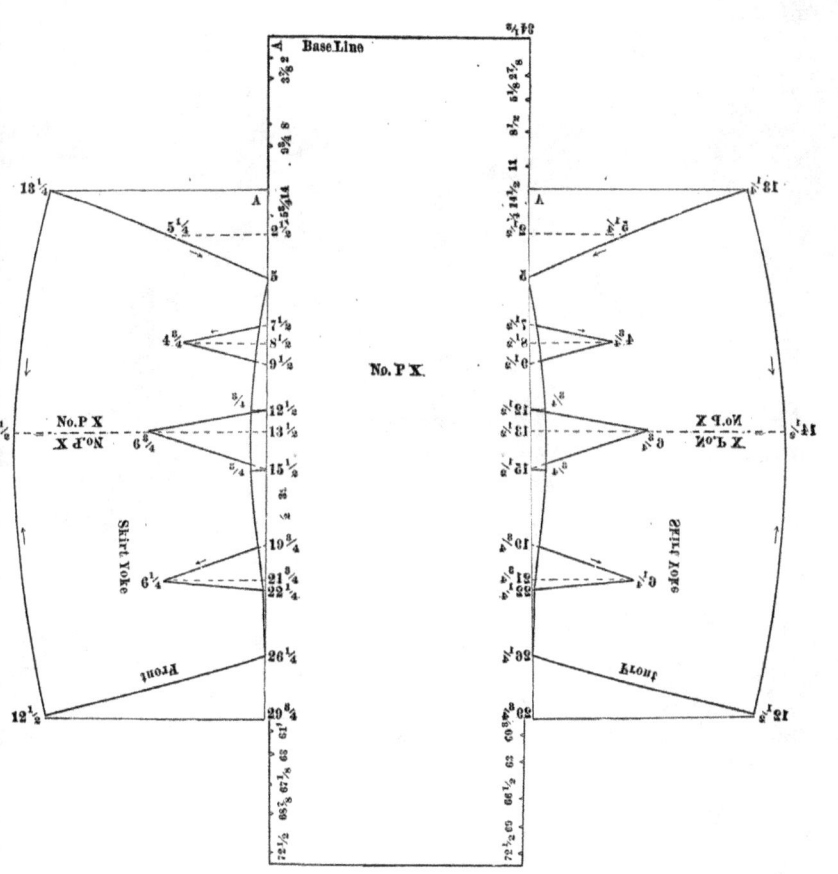

FRAYLE

Bright Eyes

No soul to sell. Desperate, dragged down & dwindling.
Maintain my grace. Swathy@souls like flies.
Dig deep. Concealed now.

Bright eyes betray a dark heart.
I don't want you to see that there's darkness in me.

I walk alone. Hiding among the empty ones.
Keeps to myself, so well veiled the misery.
Concealed. Just smile now.

Bright eyes betray a dark heart.
I don't want you to see that there's darkness in me.

So many tears, my wicked ways.
So many fears, all tucked away.

Bright eyes betray a dark heart.
I don't want you to see that there's darkness in me.

PHOTO: LENA KNOTEK

45

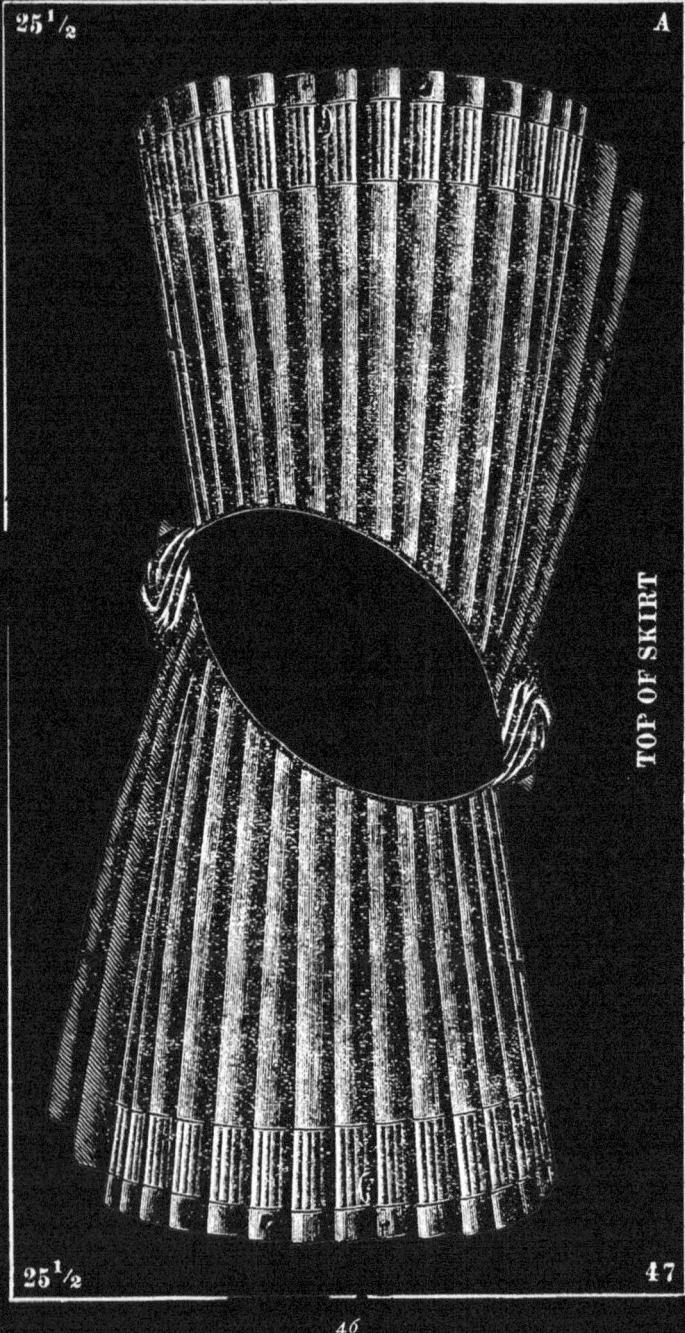

FRAYLE

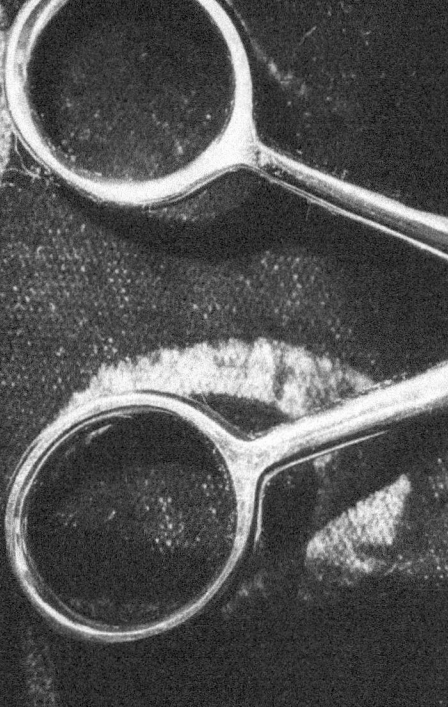

SKIN & SORROW

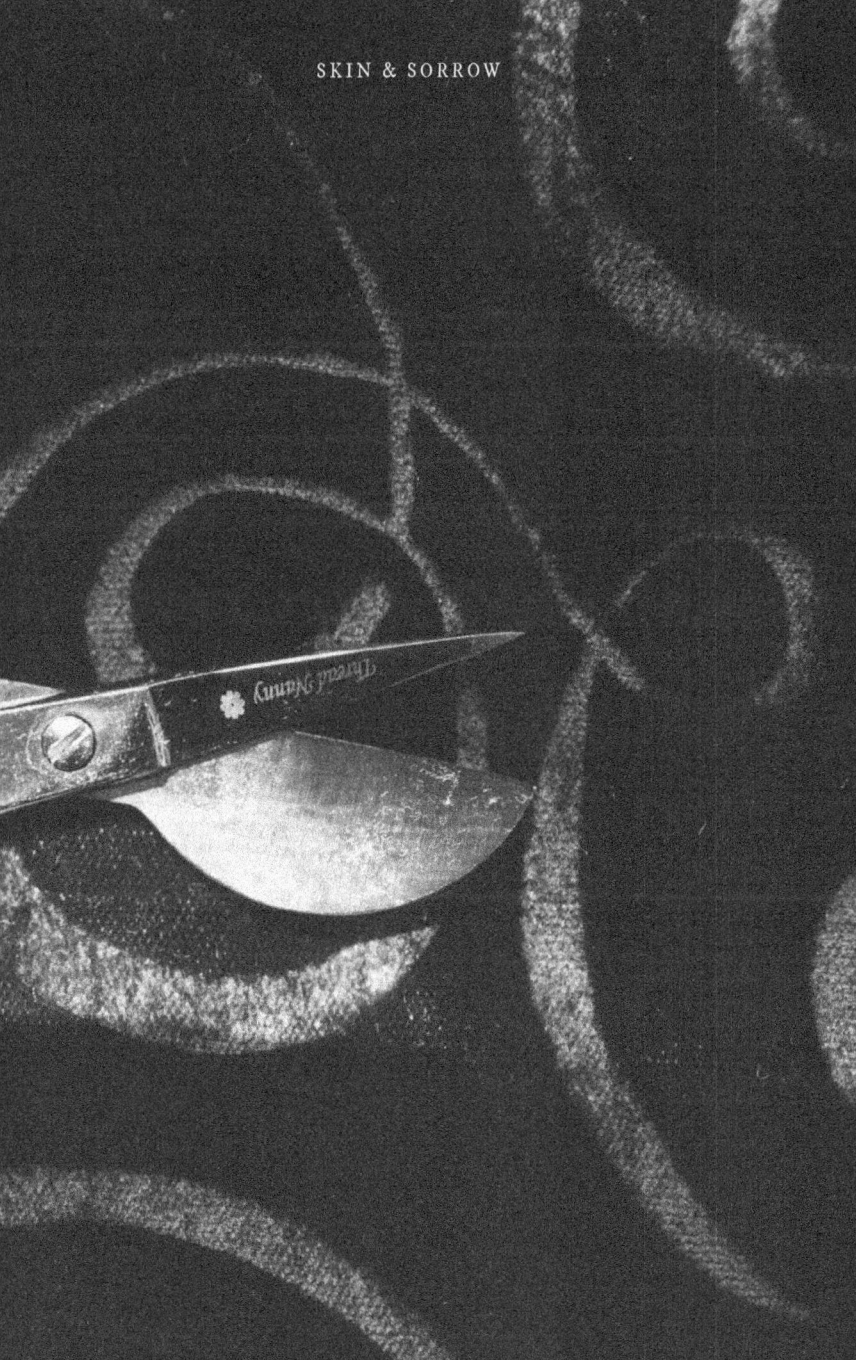

FRAYLE

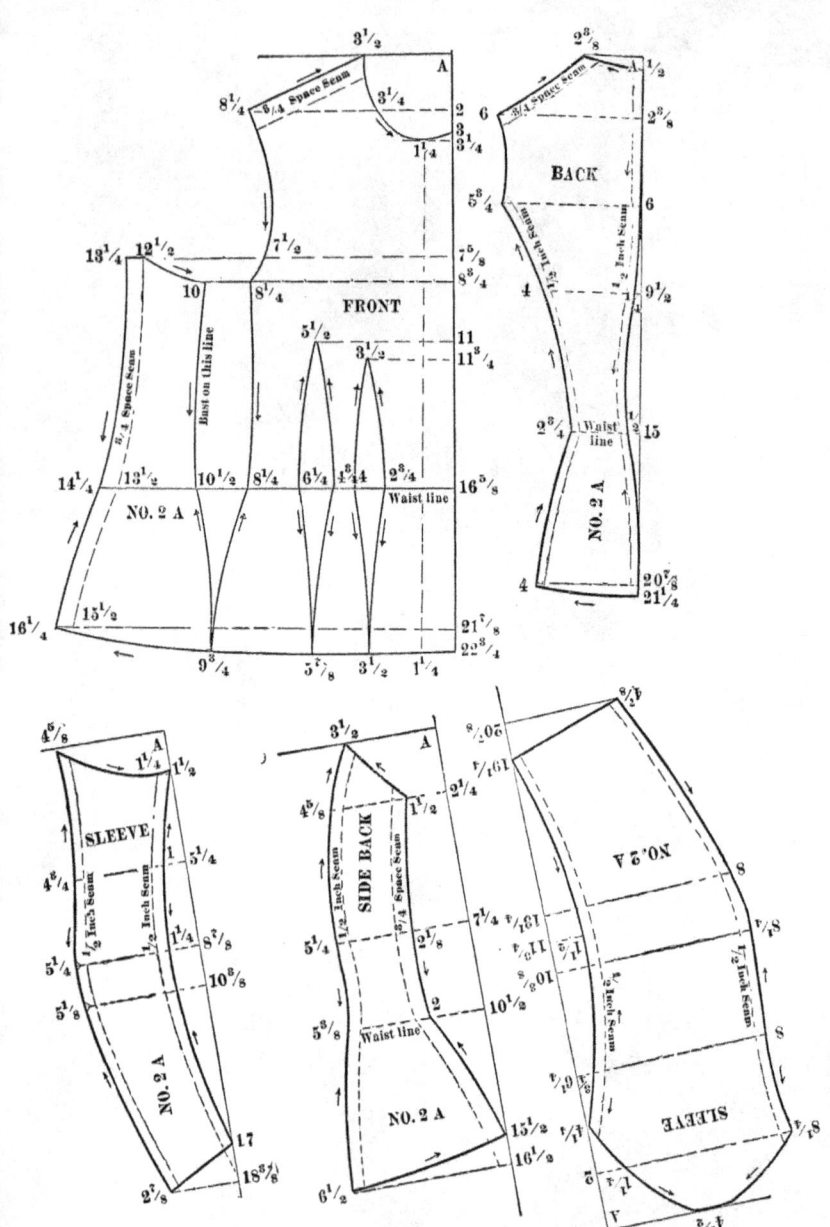

SKIN AND SORROW

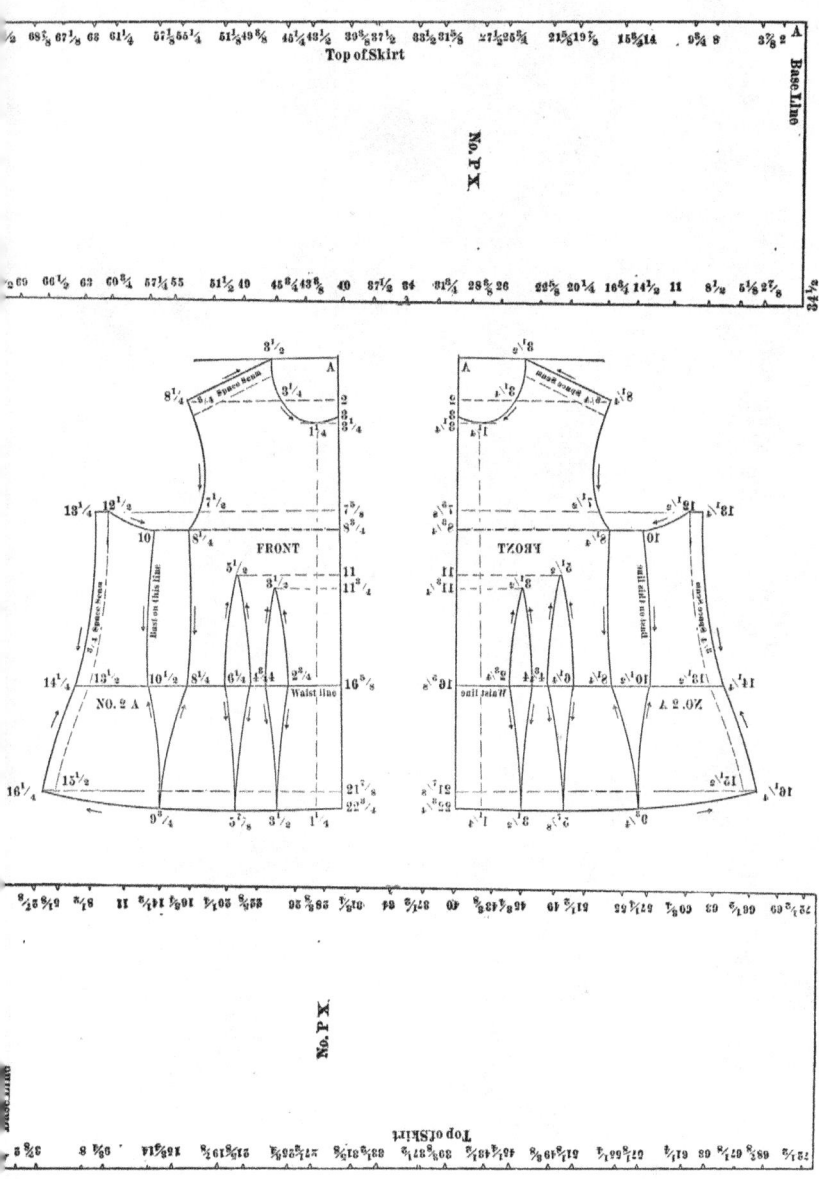

FRAYLE

Skin & Sorrow

Each tear feeds a fear. Sadness I once held dear.
Single, ragged breath swells in the dance of death.
Hide your Eyes. Hide your Eyes.

All skin & sorrow we stand, lament the hours not spent.
Held by grieving hand. Poetry written, not sent.

Invested in your misery. Mourning await your injury.
You with the broken wing, bandage your heart & sing.
Hide your eyes. Hide your eyes.

All skin & sorrow you stand, lament the hours not spent.
Held by a grieving hand. Poetry written, not sent.

I remember the night you blessed me with your eyes.
Rest now, beautiful soul.
I remember the night you blessed me with your eyes.
Bless me, beautiful soul.

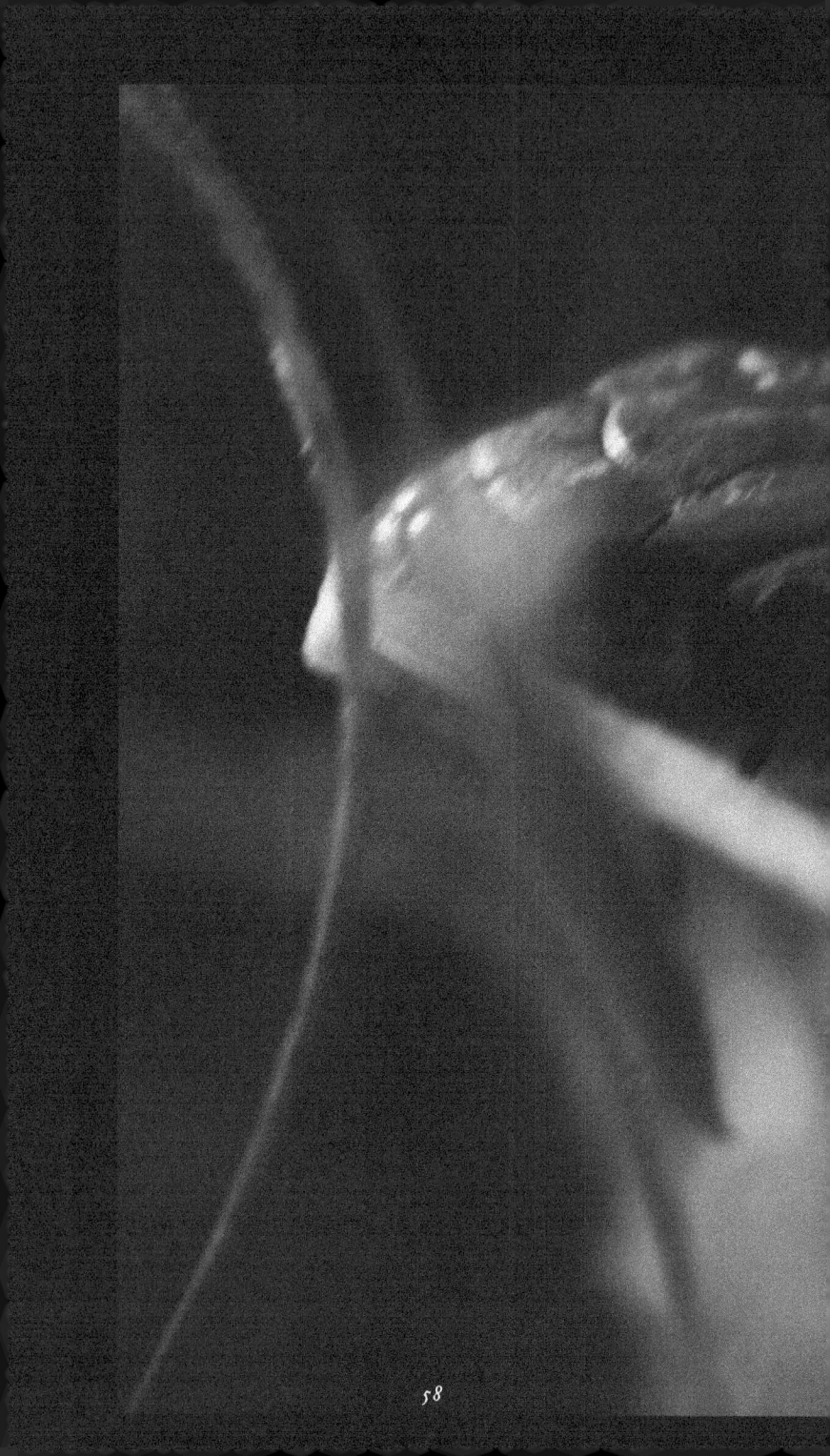
58

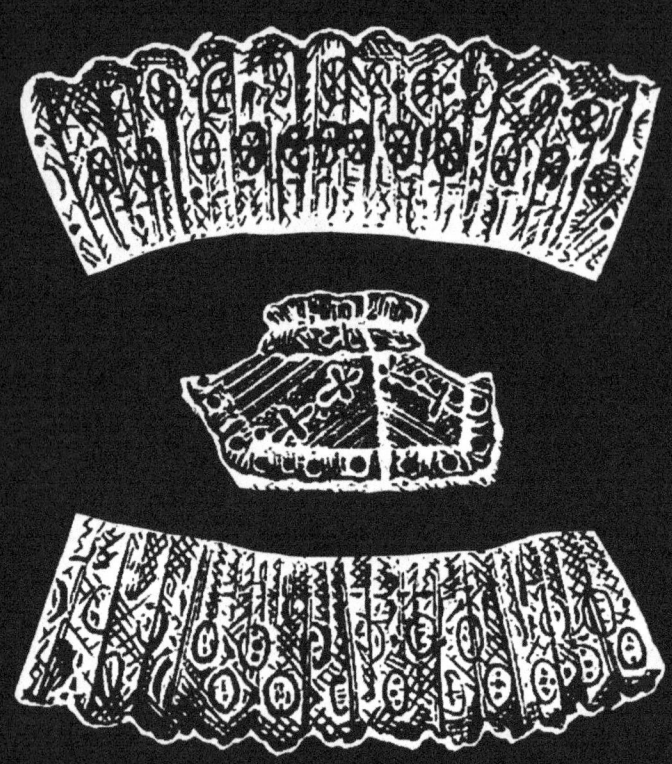

SKIN & SORROW

Ipecac

I hung you high from a cross, to hear your
sweet heartbeat fade.
Reeks of mediocrity, & the heavens it weighs.

Would you forgive my sins if I ever asked you to?
You know I carry your kiss. Say my
name, I'll run you through.

Bitter & jaded, hurtful & faded.
Such a pretty waste. Can't stand the taste of Ipecac.

I laid you softly in the dirt to watch your pale
roots grow.
Nothing special in your skin. Light falls dim
amidst shadows.

I live among the hardened few, hide among
the vacancies.
Laying while you come unglued.
Malleable decencies.

Bitter & jaded, hurtful & faded.
Such a pretty waste. Can't stand the taste of Ipecac.

You gave me almost everything.
Wrote me songs that broke my heart.
Gave me voice & made me sing.
Now, make me stop before I start.

Bitter & jaded, hurtful & faded.
Such a pretty waste, can't stand the taste of Ipecac.

FRAYLE

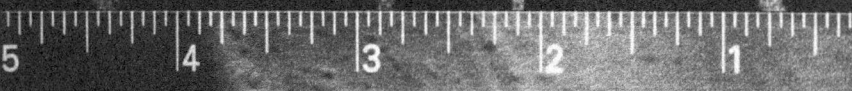

SKIN & SORROW

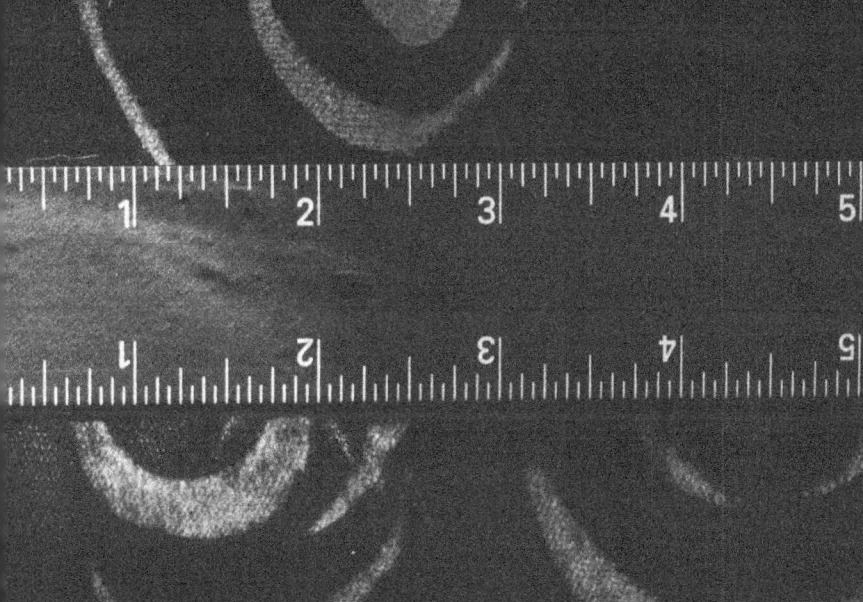

FRAYLE

✦ Stars ✦

The darkness has returned. It never really left.
This pain around me burns like a flame upon my chest.

Forever wasn't promised, but I'd swear it
was implied.

Even the stars weep at their loss.

I'll bleed for you. Mourn hands not held.
Just rest now.

Beneath this veil I try to hide the grief I bear.
I feel so very frail. Yes, I have for quite a while.

Forever wasn't promised, but I'd swear it was implied.
Even the stars weep at their loss.

I'll bleed for you. Mourn ~~hands~~ moments lost.
Just rest now.

I'll weep for you. Mourn moments lost.
Just sleep now.

FRAYLE

SKIN & SORROW

FRAYLE

82

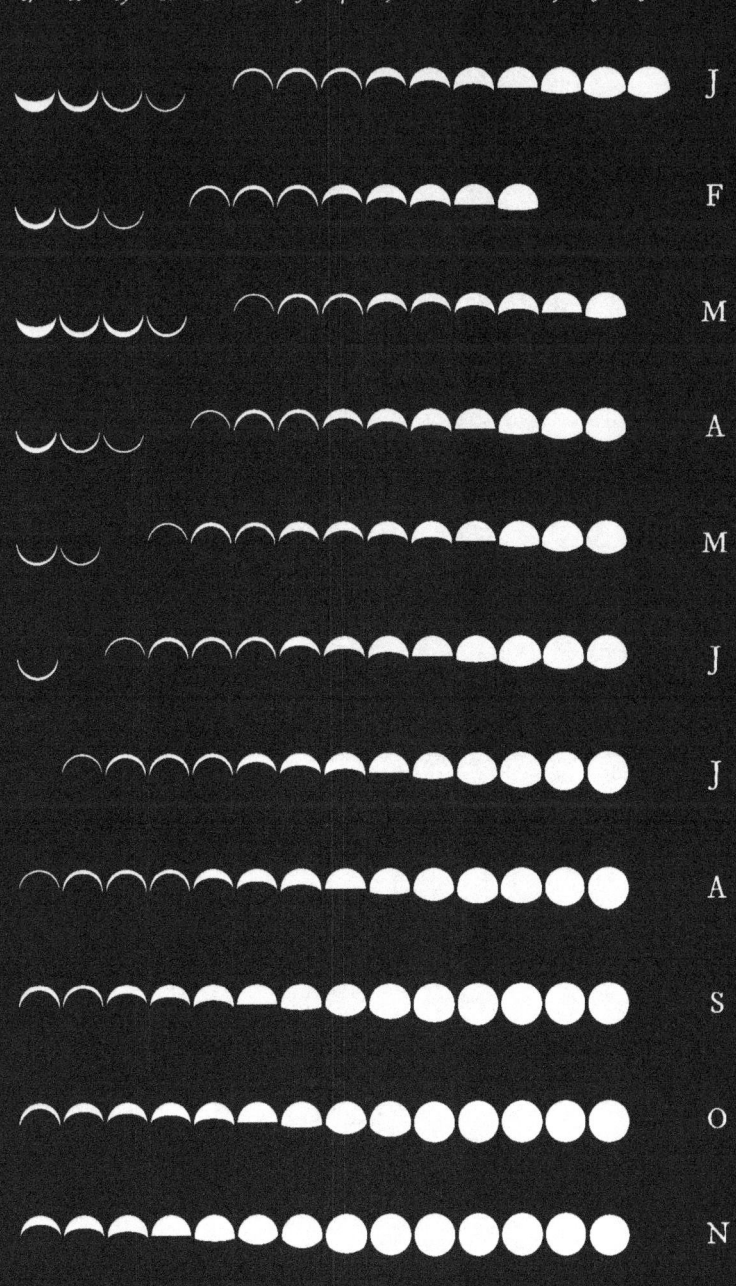

SKIN & SORROW

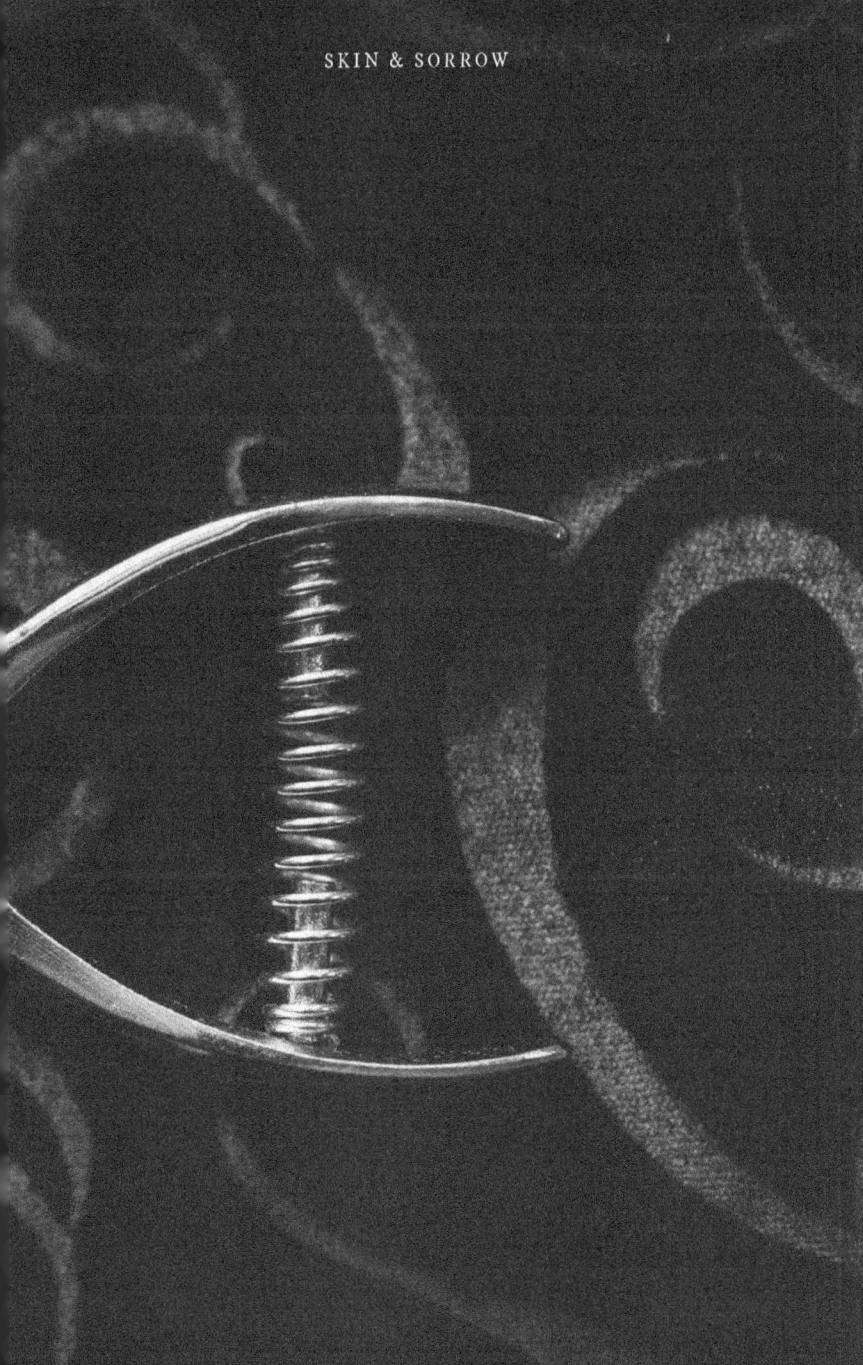

FRAYLE

Roses.

I'll send you roses, & I'll take my time.
You, you'll be the one, you'll see.
And I'll make you mine.

Some love requires roses, I prefer the thorns.
I promise to leave a beautiful scar.

Won't allow your tears to dry, & I'll pick your bones.
You, I'll bleed you dry, my love
And I'll take my fill.

Some love requires roses, I prefer the thorns
I promise to leave a beautiful scar.

Tie you up in ribbons. I'll make you mine.

Feed you my poison, & I'll stain your soul.

Some love requires roses, I prefer the thorns.
I promise to leave a beautiful scar.

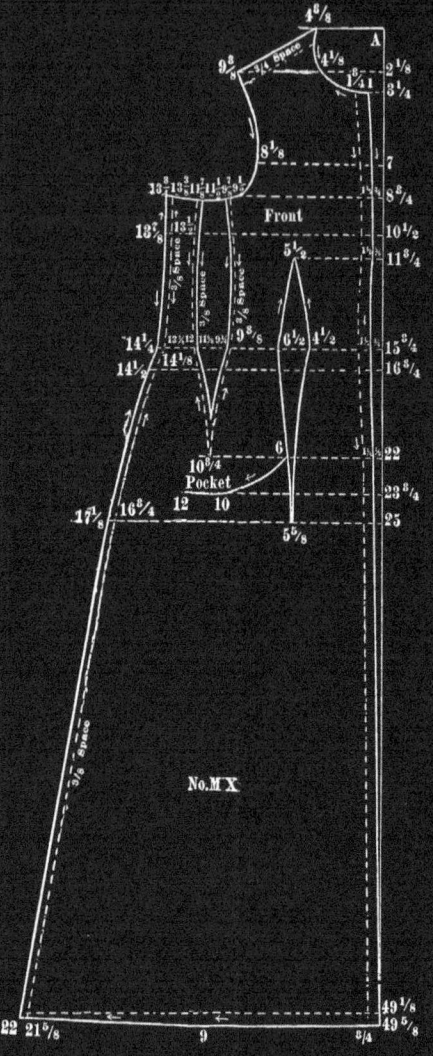
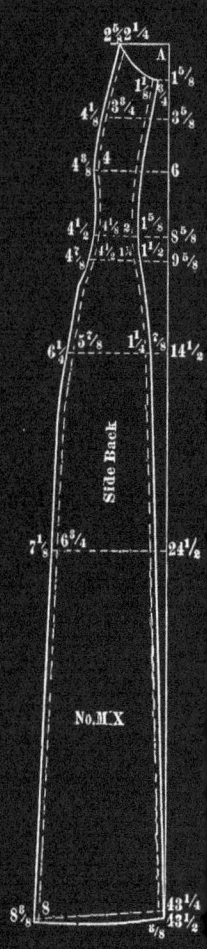

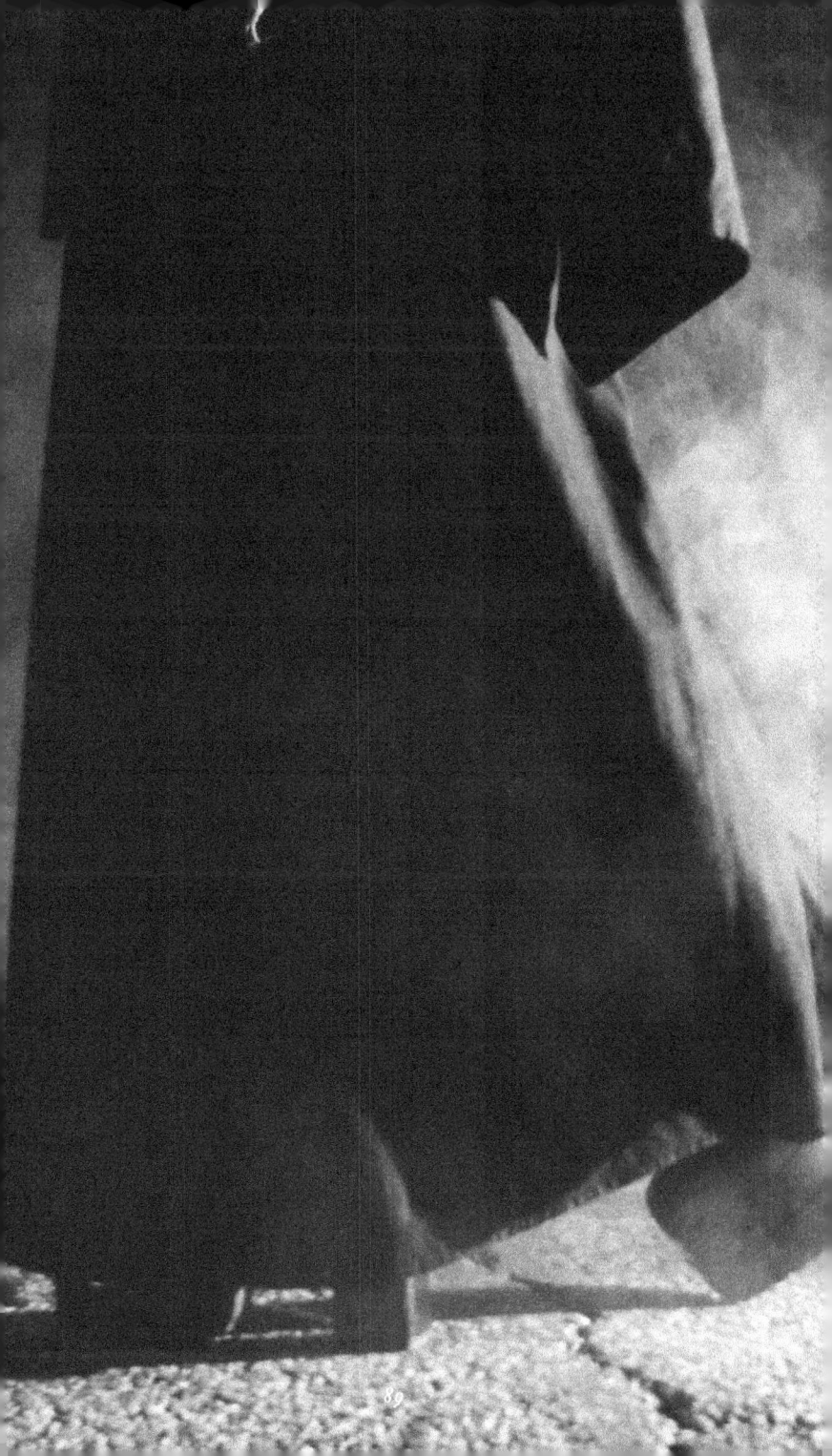

SKIN & SORROW

PHOTO: LENA KNOTEK

FRAYLE

SKIN & SORROW

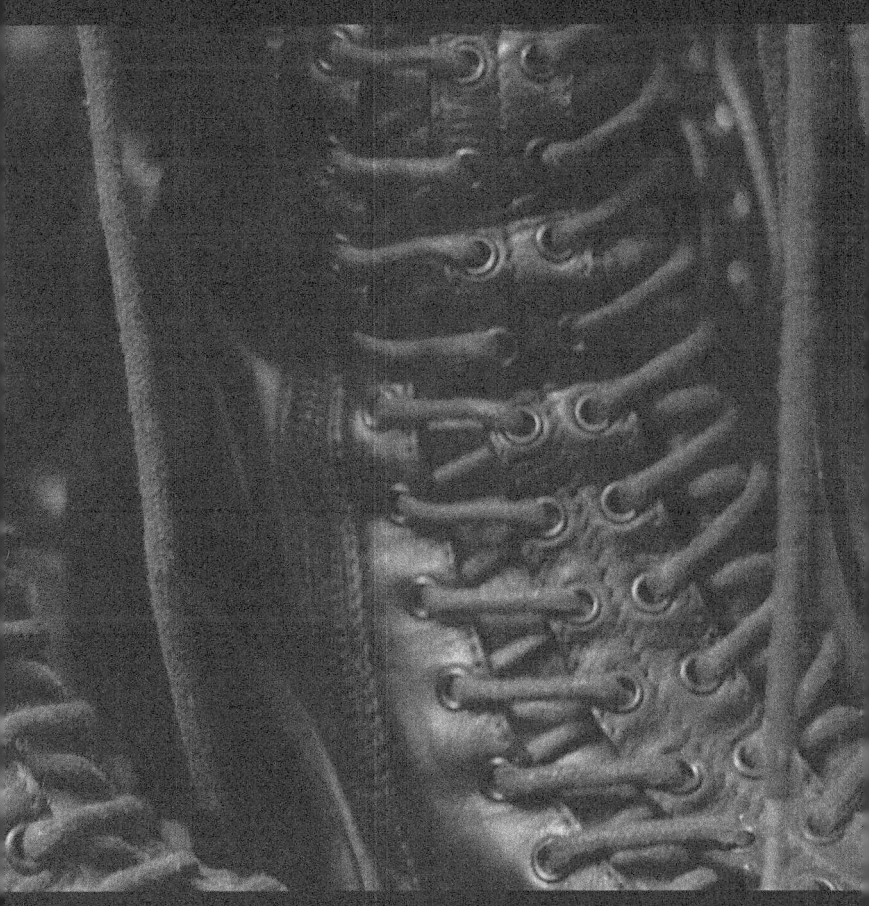

SKIN & SORROW

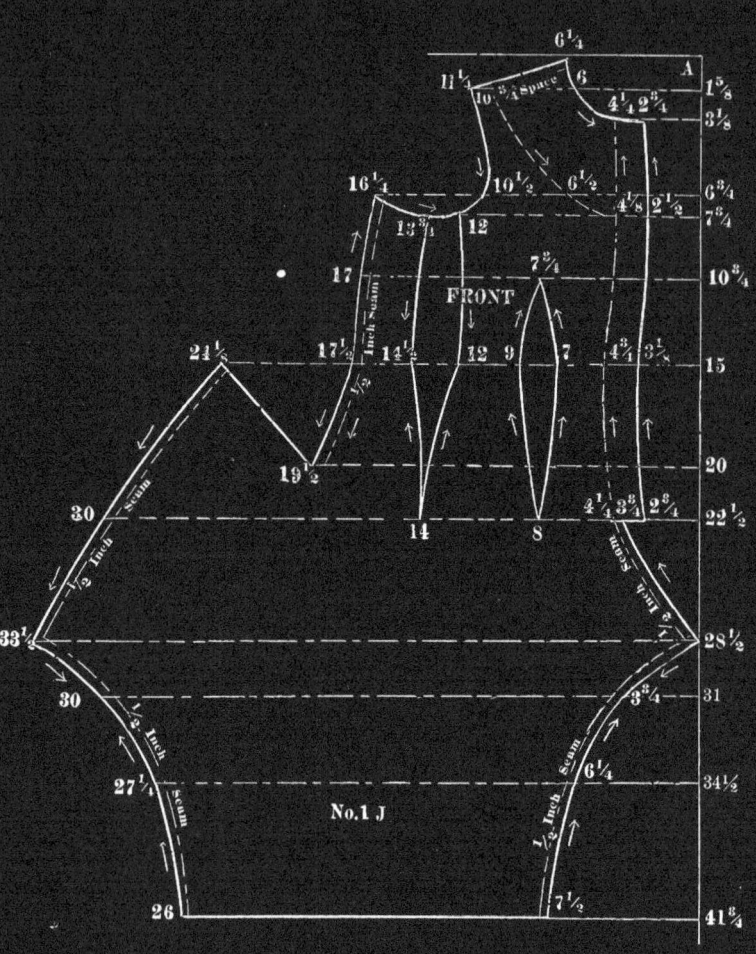

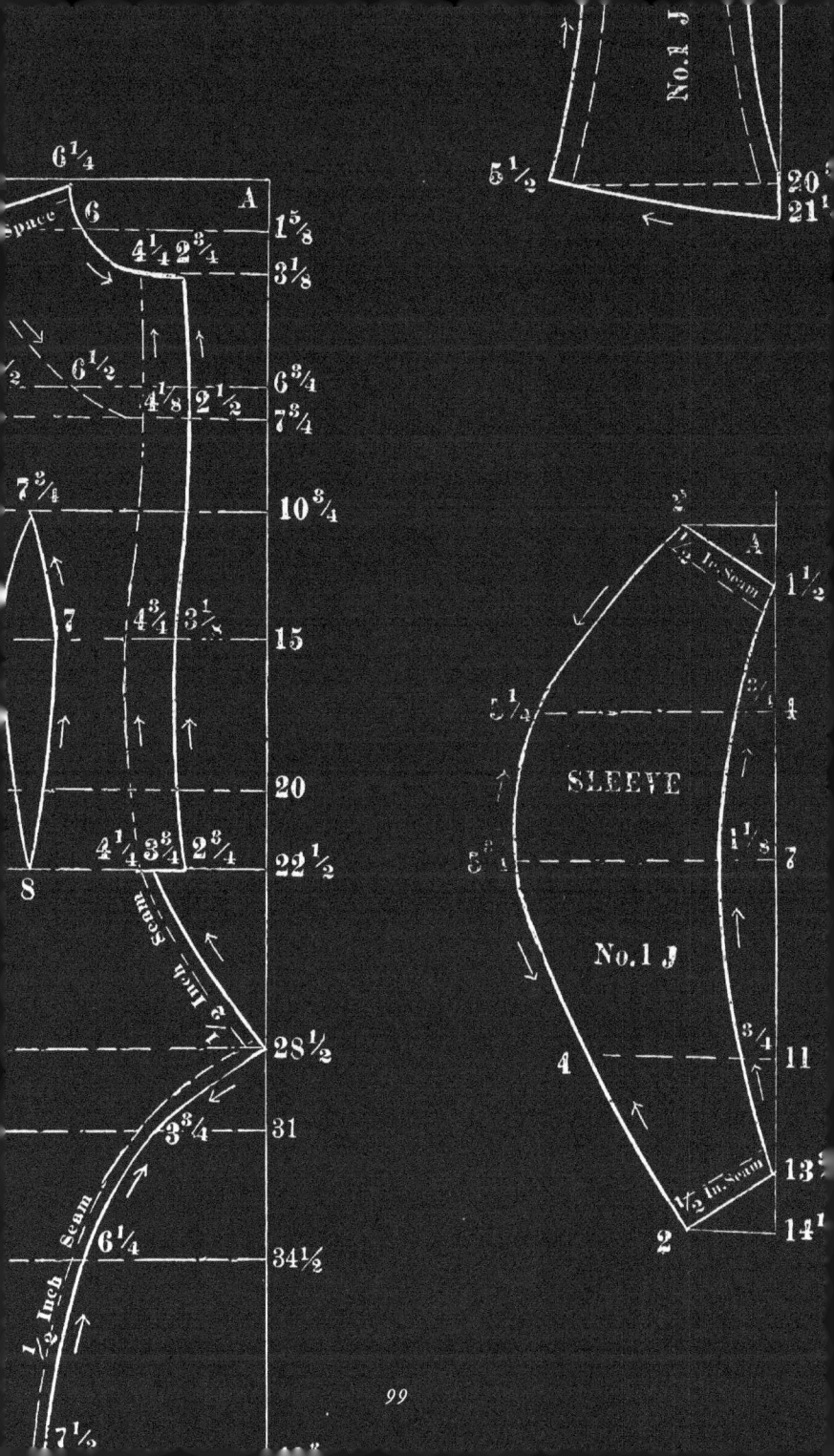

SKIN & SORROW

FRAYLE

M LANCE™

FRAYLE

SKIN & SORROW

Sacrifant

You made me bleed, I'll watch you burn.
Down on your knees, now it's your turn.

Pick @ the scab. I'll taste your tears.
Heavy hits the hand of harm.

You smell like lies, so insignificant.
I've cut all ties. Enter the sacrifant.

Pick @ the scabs. I'll taste your tears.
Heavy hits the hand of harm.

You're a wound that won't heal.
The toxicity of bitter tears run down my
cheeks & sting my lips.
I've severed my tongue.

You're the sick in my mouth

SKIN & SORROW

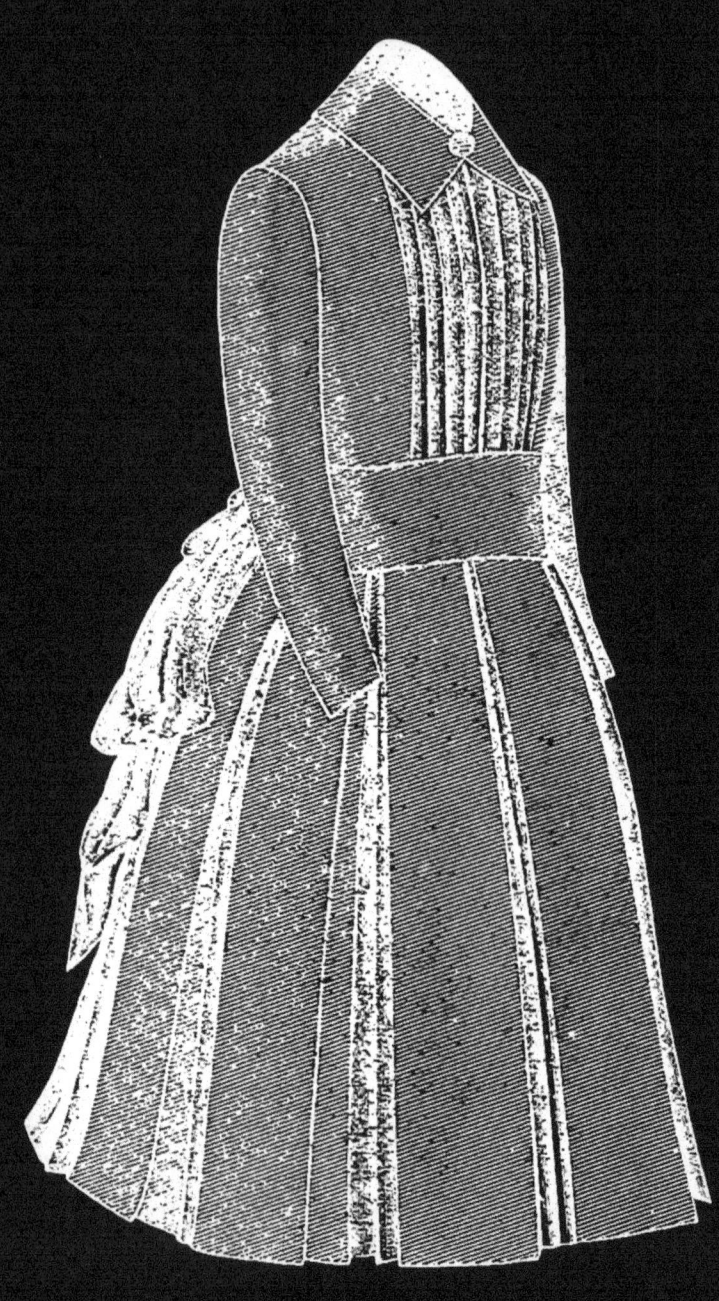

108

109

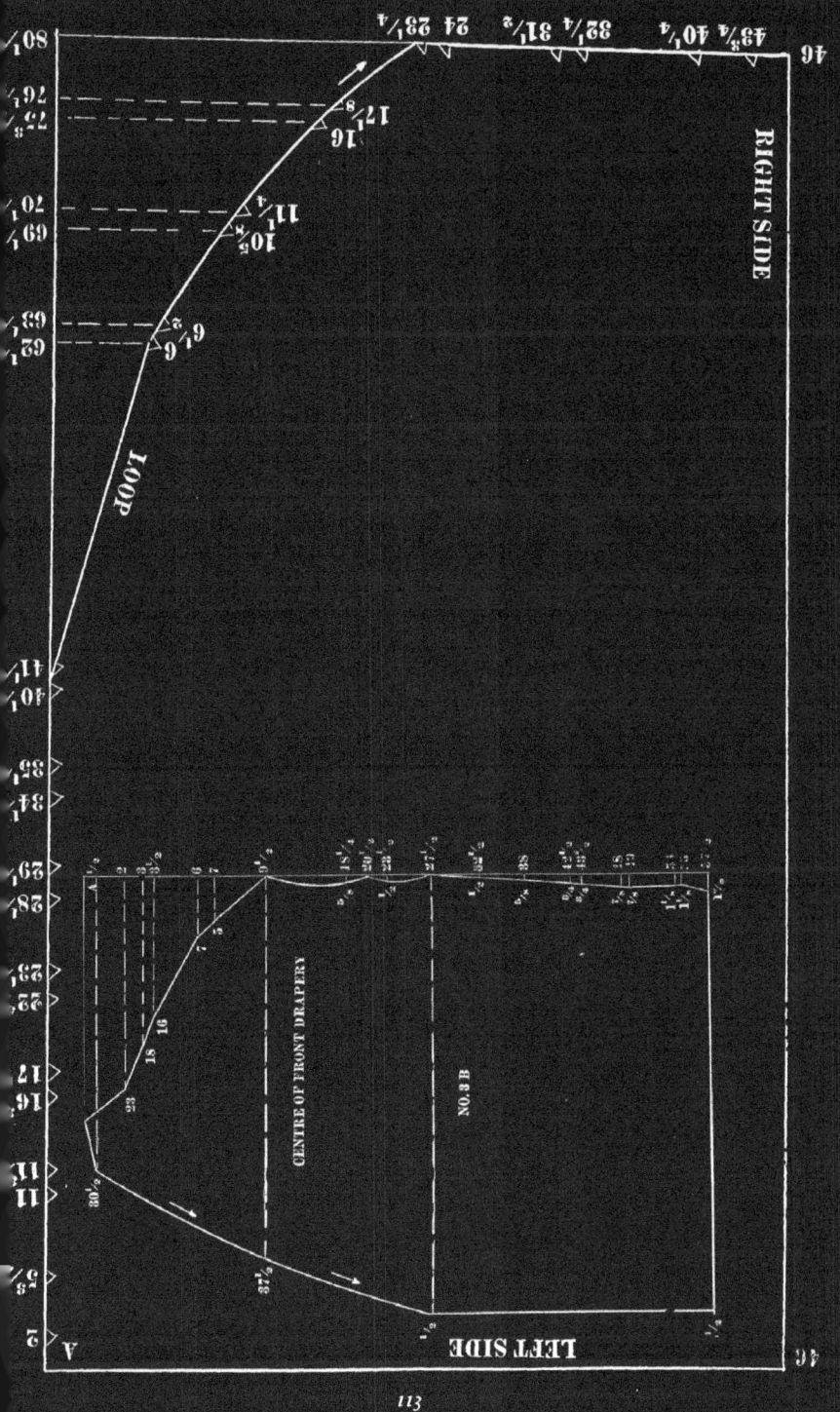

FRAYLE

SKIN & SORROW

FRAYLE

SKIN & SORROW

FRAYLE

All The Things I Was...

Gave away my pain my loss, no one's gain.
Steeped in regret, gave away my name.
Lost my identity. Center of gravity.
I left my light inside your eyes.

In your eyes. In your eyes.

Through the eyes of the joyless, I saw my goodbye.
Bright hearts are broken freely, enveloped by your sigh.

Heart full of white lies. Head down, traumatized.
Shame, what a mess, angry bitterness
Blinded by daylight. Comfort in darkness.
I left my light inside your eyes.

In your eyes. In your eyes.

Through the eyes of the joyless, I saw my goodbye.
Bright hearts are broken freely, enveloped by your sigh.

All the things I was. All the things I was.

Through the eyes of the joyless, I saw my goodbye.
Bright hearts are broken freely, enveloped by your sigh.

FRAYLE

SKIN & SORROW

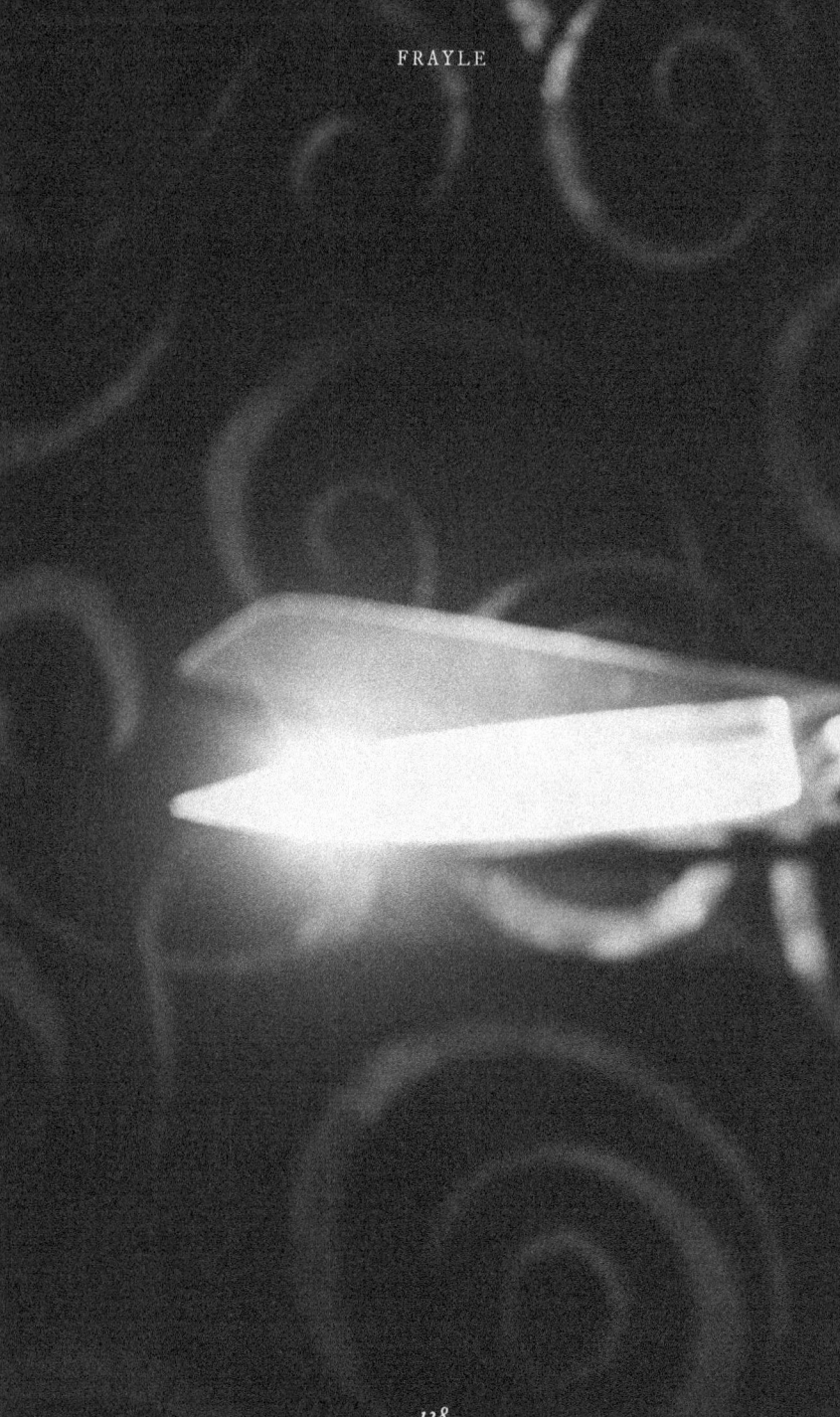

SKIN & SORROW

FRAYLE

Song For The Dead.

She sings for the dead, only.
Drawing down the moon, slowly.
Those who walk through the fire must return.

Bless those who bless us
Sing hymns for your dead.
Surrender to it.
Pray to light your light.

She walks in magick, slowly
Sings the songs of love, only
And then we all fall, freely.

Bless those who bless us.
Sing hymns for your dead.
Surrender to it.
Pray to light your light.

FRAYLE

SKIN & SORROW

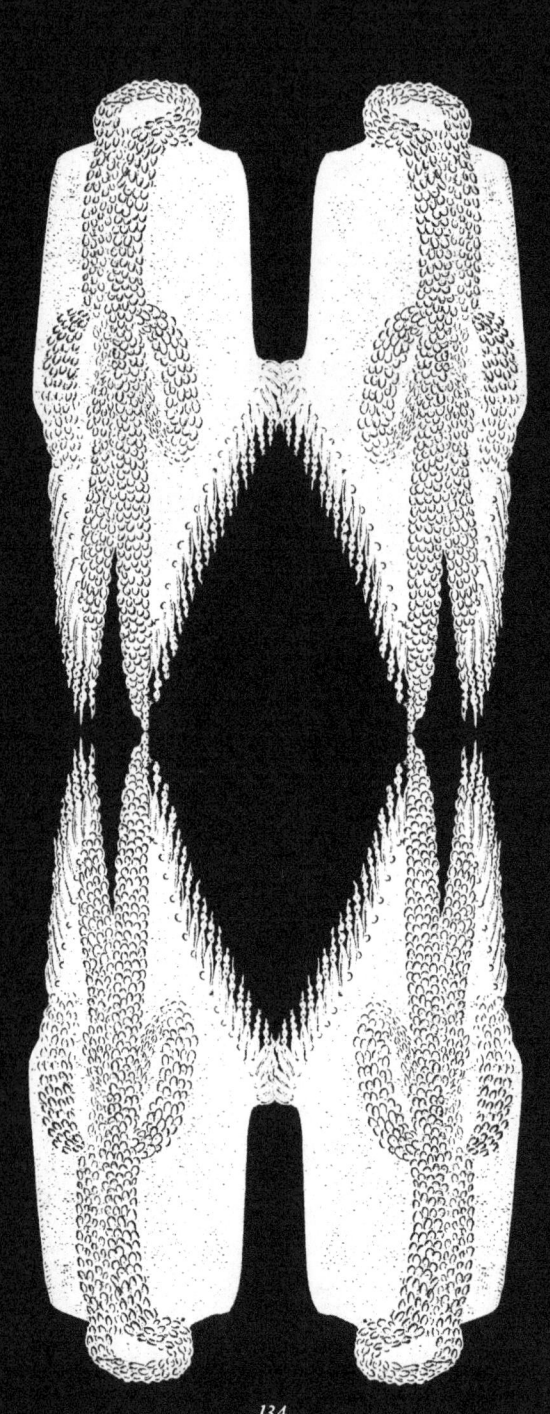

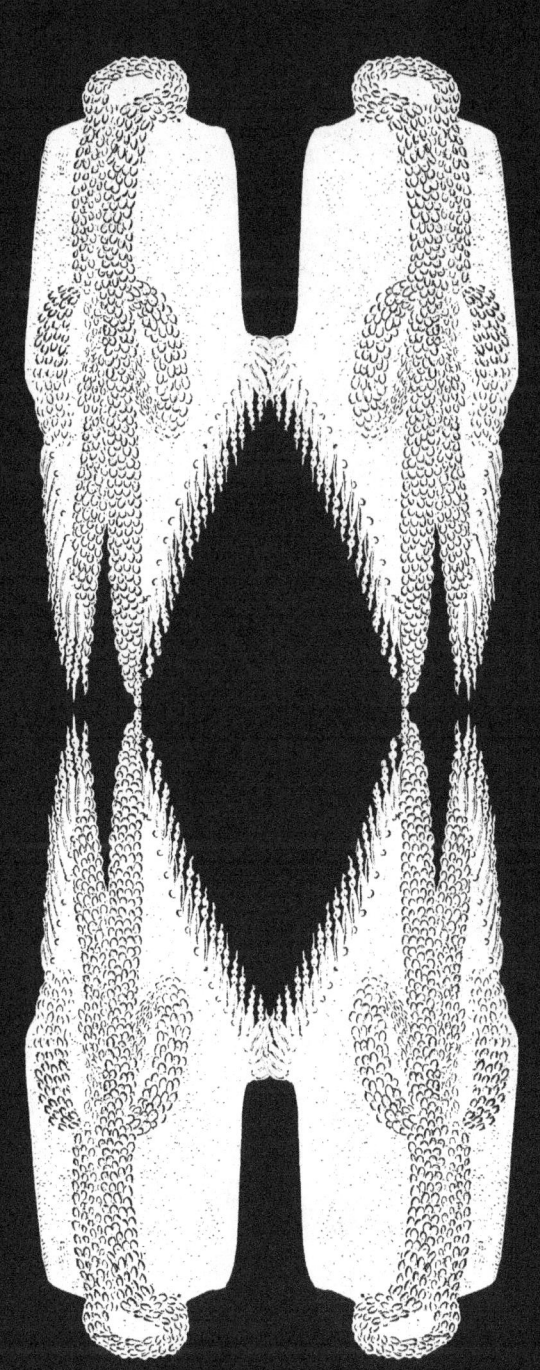

SKIN & SORROW

SKIN & SORROW

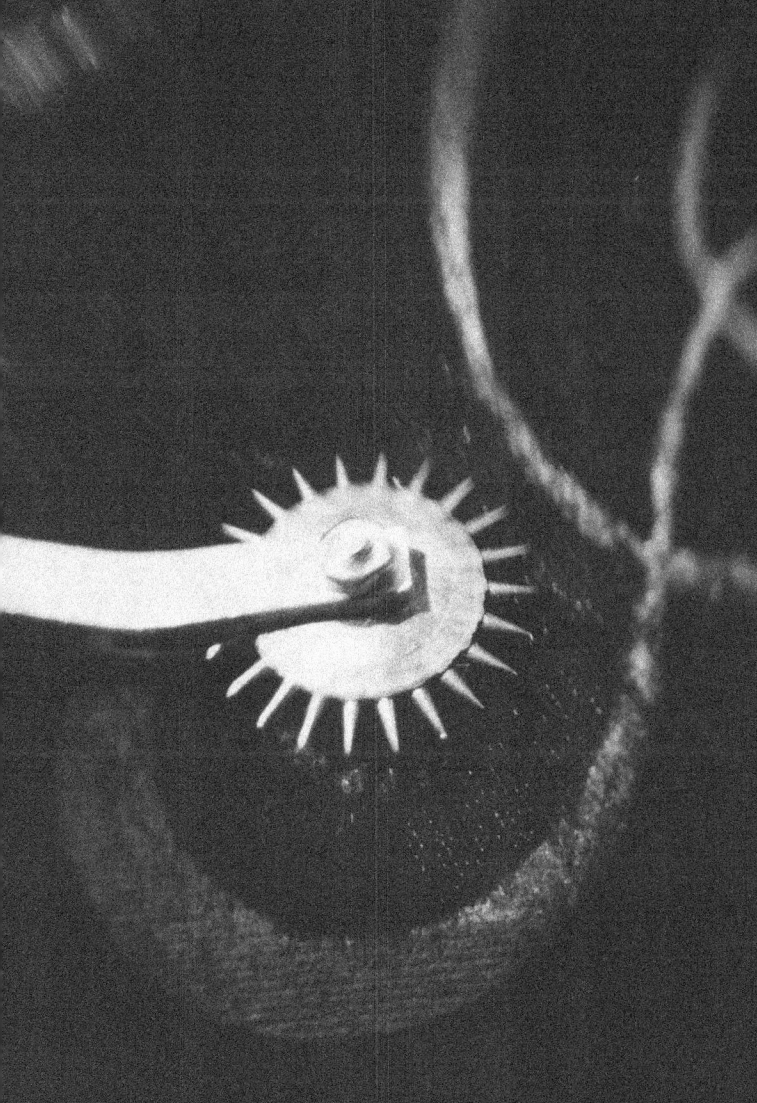

FRAYLE

Perfect Word.

My perfect misery
Breathy deep, feeling lost.
Weary, withered, mostly frail
Your tired spirit fails

My beautiful sorrow. My beautiful sorrow.

My perfect word, my sorrow
Darkness creeps in
Shine your light down on me.
Shadowed deep, feeling low.

My beautiful sorrow. My beautiful sorrow.

Want any prizes thrown
Tear the angst flat sleeps
Unknowing & unbowed
Fashionless & steep

My beautiful sorrow. My beautiful sorrow.

FRAYLE

SKIN & SORROW

SKIN & SORROW

PHOTO: LENA KNOTEK

SKIN & SORROW

FRAYLE

THE END

ALSO Available from Aqualamb Artists

- **DESCENDER** by Descender (ALR 001)
  6 song debut EP. Available formats: Digipak CD, digital / streaming
  90's Influenced post-hardcore. RIYL: Snapcase, Helmet, Quicksand
  "Angularly aggressive hardcore that takes an abrasive shape on purpose." — CMJ

- **AND SO WE MARCHED** by Descender (ALR 002)
  4 song EP. Available formats: Printed book, digital / streaming
  90's Influenced post-hardcore. RIYL: Snapcase, Helmet, Quicksand
  "...a 21st Century compliant post-hardcore band that was raised on metal and got dosed with a tab of AmRep..." — Jaded Scenster

- **TAKING DRUGS TO MAKE MUSIC TO SELL CARS TO** by Human Highlight Reel (ALR 003)
  4 song debut EP. Available formats: Vinyl record, printed book, digital / streaming
  Instrumental post-rock. RIYL: Maserati, June of 44, Russian Circles
  "Aces instrumental post rock. Think Russian Circles or perhaps a more metal Seam..." — Jaded Scenster

- **JUDGE** by Vagina Panther (ALR 004)
  5 song EP. Available formats: Printed book, digital / streaming
  Heavy female-fronted garage rock. RIYL: QOTSA, Cheeseburger, Fu Manchu, Stooges
  "Vagina Panther rocks." — Billboard

- **BLACK BLACK BLACK** by Black Black Black (ALR 005)
  12 song debut LP. Available formats: Vinyl record, printed book, digital / streaming
  Melodic death rock. RIYL: Akimbo, Torche, Lungfish, Black Flag
  "Brooklyn-by-way-of-Ohio doomsters offer up a big, nasty salute to gas tanks and goat hooves. It all coalesces to form one ravaging feast of melodic death rock that will satiate all your salacious needs, be it Nether-deity worshipping or rock star living." — Broken Beard

- **GODMAKER** by Godmaker (ALR 007)
  4 song debut LP. Available formats: Vinyl record, printed book, digital / streaming
  Doomy sludge metal. RIYL: High on Fire, Red Fang, Mastodon, The Sword
  "An example of genuine out-of-nowhere brilliance. A patient drawn out campaign of aggression." — Relix

- **THE SPACE MERCHANTS** by The Space Merchants (ALR 008)
  8 song debut LP. Available formats: Printed book, digital / streaming
  Whiskey-soaked space-rock. RIYL: Black Mountain, Dead Meadow, The Besnard Lakes
  "A unique brand of lo-fi psych rock... their huge-yet-minimal sound, mixing psych with blues and country style riffs to make something great." — Magnet

- **HIRAM-MAXIM** by Hiram-Maxim (ALR 009)
  4 song debut LP. Available formats: Vinyl record, printed book, digital / streaming
  Noisy experimental doomgaze. RIYL: Swans, Suicide, Pink Floyd, Oxbow
  "Builds into an apocalyptic fervor before dissipating into a cloudy haze & ending before you've had your fill." — VICE

- **ALTERED STATES OF DEATH AND GRACE** by Black Black Black (ALR 010)
  10 song sophomore LP. Available formats: Vinyl record, printed book, digital / streaming
  Melodic death rock. RIYL: Akimbo, Torche, Lungfish, Black Flag
  "...the kind of good-natured misanthropy of bands like Whores or KEN mode, but the musical gestures beneath the noisy exterior are all forward-charging, Kyuss-worshipping sludge n' roll. It's basically underground metal's version of a radio banger." — BrooklynVegan

- **TRESPASSES** by Nathaniel Shannon & The Vanishing Twin (ALR 011)
  15 song debut LP. Available formats: Printed book, digital / streaming
  Unsettling bedroom recording darkness. RIYL: Lanegan, Badalemnti, Springsteen, Waits
  "An unsettling yet captivating collection of songs compiled from a decade of bedroom recordings... Shannon's spoken word-style vocals over haunting and minimalist instrumentals lend a creepy atmosphere to the record." — Decibel

☐ **FERA by Husbandry** (ALR 012)
8 song debut LP. Available formats: Printed book, CD, digital / streaming
Female-fronted math rock meets post-hardcore. RIYL: Mars Volta, Glassjaw, Refused, Deftones
"It's hard to believe that Husbandry is not the biggest band in the world. They're heavy and mathy, chaos wrapped in hard rock and heavy metal." – Nerdist

☐ **MURDEREDMAN by MURDEREDMAN** (ALR 013)
8 song sophomore LP. Available formats: Vinyl record, printed book, digital / streaming
Post-punk inspired noise rock. RIYL: Savages, Bauhaus, Boris, Killing Joke
"A patient and disciplined examination of anxiety and melancholy underpinned with a cathartic tension-and-release structure that borrows from goth, post-metal, and no-wave..." – New Noise Magazine

☐ **IN TENSIONS by Lo-Pan** (ALR 014)
5 song EP. Available formats: Vinyl record, printed book, CD, digital / streaming
Anthemic desert rock. RIYL: Soundgarden, ASG, Torche, Red Fang
"Calling Lo-Pan a stoner band is a disservice to the amalgam of influences the band successfully merges together: the soulful alt rock of the 90s with a thundering doom/sludge sound that's equal parts immediate and timeless." – Nine Circles

☐ **GHOSTS by Hiram-Maxim** (ALR 015)
7 song LP. Available formats: Vinyl record, printed book, digital / streaming
Noisy experimental doomgaze. RIYL: Swans, Suicide, Pink Floyd, Oxbow
"Everything is awash in mesmerizing ambient skree and squalls of atonal feedback. Think an extended, updated version of side 2 of Black Flag's My War." – Hellride Music

☐ **KISS THE DIRT by The Space Merchants** (ALR 016)
10 song sophomore LP. Available formats: Vinyl record, printed book, digital / streaming
Whiskey-soaked space-rock. RIYL: Black Mountain, Dead Meadow, The Besnard Lakes
"[T]he sonic equivalent of having an acid trip in the bathroom between Woodstock and a ZZ Top concert in '69" – New Noise Magazine

☐ **BAD WEEDS NEVER DIE by Husbandry** (ALR 017)
5 song EP. Available formats: Printed book, CD, digital / streaming
Female-fronted math rock meets post-hardcore. RIYL: Mars Volta, Glassjaw, Refused, Deftones
"While retaining their bold go-anywhere style, the EP is a more streamlined and focused effort, signaling a greater maturity and command of recording." – Echoes and Dust

☐ **BY THE GRACE OF BLOOD AND GUTS by Haan** (ALR 018)
8 song LP. Available formats: Printed book, Vinyl, CD, digital / streaming
Noise, Grime, Sludge, Metal, Rock. RIYL: Unsane, Melvins, Swans, Helmet, Clutch
"If Melvins and Unsane had a kid while under the influence of hallucinogens" – Metal Insider

☐ **LUMINOUS VOLUMES by Skryptor** (ALR 019)
7 song LP. Available formats: Vinyl, Printed book, CD, digital / streaming
Noise, Math rock, Prog. RIYL: craw, Dazzling Killmen, Don Caballero
"Galloping, off-kilter and unabashedly victorious, proggy noise-rock outfit Skryptor's takes hard-rock/psychedelic throwback tropes, flips them on their heads and stretches it all into an adventurous march through endlessly shifting soundscapes."" – Revolver

☐ **DEAD INSIDE by Frayle** (ALR 021)
7 song 7". Alchemy Box: Printed book, Vinyl, CD, digital / streaming
Heavy witch doom. RIYL: Chelsea Wolfe, Portis Head, Sleep, Sunn O)))
"Trades in dark psychedelics and heavy, dripping drums that punctuate the riffing that plays in and around vocalist Gywn Strang's superb voice." – Nine Circles

☐ **SUBTLE by Lo-Pan** (ALR 022)
11 song LP. Available formats: Vinyl, Printed book, CD, digital / streaming
Anthemic desert rock. RIYL: Soundgarden, ASG, Torche, Red Fang
Subtle was produced by James Brown (NIN, Foo Fighters, Ghost) and mastered by Ted Jensen (Mastodon, Deftones, Bad Company, GNR).

- [ ] **1692 by Frayle** (ALR 023)
  8 song LP. Available formats: Vinyl, Printed book, CD, digital / streaming
  Heavy witch doom. RIYL: Chelsea Wolfe, Portishead, Sleep
  "Haunting, hypnotic mix of crushing Sleep-style doom and cooing ethereal vocals a la Cocteau Twins' Elizabeth Fraser." – Revolver

- [ ] **DESTROYER DELIVER by Zeb Gould** (ALR 024)
  8 song LP. Available formats: Printed book, CD, digital / streaming
  Indie-style gloom-folk meets fingerpicking prairie-bliss. RIYL: Neil Young, Gillian Welch, Bill Callahan
  "Gould's voice along with his contributors create a sense of warmth throughout their music that makes their melancholic sound comforting and inviting. Destroyer Deliver would be a welcomed addition to any music collection looking to add some mindfulness to their space."– Northern Transimission

- [ ] **THE THREE MOTHERS by Nathaniel Shannon & the Vanishing Twin** (ALR 025)
  3 song EP. Available formats: Limited Edition Cassette Box, digital / streaming
  THE THREE MOTHERS is a primordial fixation with Dario Argento's trilogy's witches. RIYL: Lanegan, Badalemnti, Springsteen, Tom Waits
  "There are very few times that you listen to music and it's something brand new. Something that has it's own identity and style. Nathaniel Shannon's new EP delivers a passionate dark dreamscape of life. His leathery dark vocals are ominous as the music that he creates. Close your eyes and you're suddenly walking down a street with faceless people and distant sound of sirens."– Steve Austin (Today is the Day / Austin Enterprises)

- [ ] **PRISONER'S CINEMA by Burning Tongue** (ALR 026)
  11 song LP. Available formats: Vinyl, Printed book, CD, digital / streaming
  Crushing nihilism that nod to the shadowy side of hardcore punk. RIYL: Power Trip, Craft, G.I.S.M.
  "It's a furious expulsion of nihilistic metallic hardcore, racing and ravaging, clanging and clobbering, seething and slashing." – No Clean Singing

- [ ] **THE LINE, IT'S WIDTH, AND THE WARDRONE by Rebreather** (ALR 028)
  8 song LP. Available formats: Vinyl, Printed book, digital / streaming
  Doom, Sludge, Metal, Prog. RIYL: Part Chimp, Unsane, Melvins
  "...shows that the band are more than mere noise merchants, but an outfit who know how to strike poise and balance, wringing every last drop of catharsis out of the track." – The Sleeping Shaman

- [ ] **SKIN & SORROW by Frayle** (ALR 033)
  10 song LP. Available formats: Vinyl, Printed book, CD, digital / streaming
  Heavy Witch Ritual Doom Metal. RIYL: Earth, King Woman, Portishead
  "[Frayle] create spinetingling devastation doom that curdles the blood and casts dreamy spells, with Gwyn layering gossamer-light My Bloody Valentine-esque vocals over dirgy riffs." – Metal Hammer

- [ ] **THUNDERHEADS by LaMacchia** (ALR 034)
  9 song LP. Available formats: Vinyl, Printed book, CD, digital / streaming
  Egnimatic layered & moody rock, metal and electronica. RIYL: Liars, Doves, Autolux, Radiohead
  "For every rush of adrenaline there's the eventual lull. For each euphoric high there's the comedown to follow. Thunderheads plays like the 3am winding down of a night of excess. Thrills and sensual desires wedded to a shadow of sadness and introspection." – Ghost Cult

---

JOIN THE AQUALAMB RESEARCH CLUB

A record company like Aqualamb releases many albums and books each year. Some of them are by long established artists while others are by people no one has heard of but us. In either case, we'd like to try out some of our upcoming music on you. After all you are the consumer. The final decision is always yours.

So we'd like to know what you think just a little bit earlier. You might say, we'd like to put you into our A&R Department with a little service we call Aqualamb Research Club. Aqualamb Research Club is a series of songs we'll be sending out over the course of a year. On each one you'll get a sampling of brand-new or unreleased albums. Each issue of Aqualamb Research Club comes a minimal-baloney newsletter telling you what we and our artists have been up to lately.

Your role in Aqualamb Research Club is simple. All we want is to hear from you—what you like, what you hate, and why. A year of Aqualamb Research Club will cost you 10 bucks, which just about covers packaging and mailing. In return, you will get a lot of fine music, an Aqualamb T-shirt, and a special Aqualamb Research Club pin plus the chance to influence the course of music.

The music for Frayle – *Skin & Sorrow*
can be downloaded
via the link below:

http://aqualamb.org/033

www.ingramcontent.com/pod-product-compliance
Lightning Source LLC
Chambersburg PA
CBHW051343040426
42453CB00007B/388